# YES YOU CAN!

# YES YOU CAN!

## YOUR GUIDE TO BECOMING AN ACTIVIST

### JANE DRAKE & ANN LOVE

TUNDRA BOOKS

Published in Canada by Tundra Books,
75 Sherbourne Street, Toronto, Ontario M5A 2P9

Published in the United States by Tundra Books of Northern New York,
P.O. Box 1030, Plattsburgh, New York 12901

Library of Congress Control Number: 2009938089

**Library and Archives Canada Cataloguing in Publication**

Drake, Jane
Yes you can! : your guide to becoming an
activist / Jane Drake, Ann Love.

Includes index.
ISBN 978-0-88776-942-9

1. Social change – Juvenile literature.  2. Social
action – Juvenile literature.  I. Love, Ann  II. Title.

HN18.3.D73 2010        j361.2083        C2009-905847-2

We acknowledge the financial support of the Government of Canada through the
Book Publishing Industry Development Program (BPIDP) and that of the
Government of Ontario through the Ontario Media Development Corporation's
Ontario Book Initiative.

We further acknowledge the support of the Canada Council for the Arts and the
Ontario Arts Council for our publishing program.

ONTARIO ARTS COUNCIL
CONSEIL DES ARTS DE L'ONTARIO

Design: Paul Dotey

Printed in Canada

1  2  3  4  5  6        15  14  13  12  11  10

*For the change-makers in our immediate family, whose work in social justice is a daily inspiration – Stephanie Drake, David Love, and Jennifer Love*

## Acknowledgments

With thanks to...

Mike Balkwill; Henry, Ian, and William Barnett; Patrick Barnett; Kim Beatty; Lee Ann Boop; Tim Borlase; Catherine Bradley; Barbara Cochrane; Jane Crist; Brian, Jim, and Madeline Drake; Emily Drake; Kayode Fatoba; David Furlong; John Giles; Monte Hummel; Brian and Ruth Kelly; Mikaela Lefaive; Adrian and Melanie Love; Gage Love; Geoff and Kate Love; Garfield Mahood; David Morley; Michael Perley; Evan, Luke, and Olivia Racine; Mark, Mason, and Sadie Salmoni; David Sorek; David Spedding; and Mary Thompson.

Many thanks to Kathy Lowinger and Sue Tate, who enthusiastically endorsed this book and helped us step up to a different readership. Thanks also to the Tundra team – we wouldn't change a thing about you!

## Authors' Note

In the timeline, we use modern place names, such as Iran and Italy, followed by the historical names of peoples, such as the Persians and the Spartans. Where we couldn't pinpoint an exact date, we selected one mid-timeframe and used the symbol $c$ for *circa* to indicate that our date is approximate.

# CONTENTS

## *introduction*

# STEP RIGHT UP!

Imagine a world where whalers are allowed to kill whatever moves on the high seas. Or a town where only one race of people can sit in the front seats of the bus. Or a high school where cigarette companies can market their products to students. What if young people could be thrown into prison for what they believe or for even what they wear to school? What if preteens could be forced to work in factories if their parents needed money instead of attending school?

Are these nightmare imaginings? No – these things happened in many parts of the world until recent times and, in some places, happen still. And where change has ended these nightmares, determined people made the difference. Who were these change-makers and how did they do it? Read on . . .

Maybe you, too, see something that needs to change. Or have a dream for a better world and want to work towards it. If that is you, read on . . .

This book divides the process of change into nine steps. Each step is introduced with a dramatic story of change on a major issue to highlight the step itself. Then useful strategies and skills, critical to fulfilling every step, are offered. A historical timeline of milestones and setbacks puts the magnitude of the change into context.

Start where you may be right now – *I'm Fed Up*. Has something grabbed your attention and hit you in the gut? You may feel sickened, irritated, or totally annoyed. **STEP ONE** asks you to take a breath, look inwards, and galvanize your negative feelings into positive action.

**STEP TWO** – *What's Wrong?* – helps you pinpoint the problem, research it, then state it clearly.

*Great Minds Think Alike*, **STEP THREE**, suggests you find out who is already working on the same thing and who your supporters are. What might you expect with a partnership or coalition? What are the ups and downs of working with others? How can you identify and cultivate the opposition?

A baseball personality, Branch Rickey, once said, "Luck is the residue of design." **STEP FOUR** looks at the relationship between hard work and luck in *Good Plans, Good Luck*.

Some changes come about more easily by setting one attainable goal after another. **STEP FIVE** investigates *Baby Steps, Giant Leaps*.

And when the road gets rocky, *Butting Heads* offers ways to manage a power struggle successfully in **STEP SIX**.

**STEP SEVEN**, *When the Going Gets Tough, the Tough Get Going*, helps you stick with it, even when the challenge becomes personal.

Then, **STEP EIGHT** inspires you with innovative ways of *Getting Heard* if your cause gets mired in red tape, apathy, or disinterest.

And **STEP NINE** looks at *Life after Change*, when the excitement of pioneering is over but the work must continue.

These nine steps follow a useful sequence, but the order may vary in a real campaign. Or you may be better at blazing your own trail than following someone else's template step-by-step. No matter what your style, you can be successful when you listen to your heart, develop a solid vision for a better future, and empower yourself through knowledge and action.

You can begin with a simple project – such as improving the cleanliness of the bathrooms at school, or removing invasive plants from a neighborhood park. Or you can start with a larger campaign – such as persuading your local school or community to dramatically reduce their carbon footprint. Even if you start small, you will make a difference, and you will learn how to be more effective next time.

Imagine a world where global warming has stopped; every child goes to bed well nourished; forests grow back faster than they are being cut down; people are respectful to each other; torture and war have disappeared; there are no prisoners of conscience anywhere; everyone enjoys health care, education, clean water, and fresh air – the possibilities are endless. Daydreams or future realities? Go for it!

# I'M
# FED
# UP

**P**eter Benenson was furious. On November 19, 1960, while riding the London Underground and reading the newspaper, he came across a story that shocked his deepest, personal ideals.

A lawyer, Peter believed fiercely in the rights and freedoms of all people. An Englishman, he was proud of his country's part in formulating the United Nations Universal Declaration of Human Rights. That declaration, passed twelve years earlier, asserted the rights held by every person on Earth, including the right to freedom of speech. Peter knew cruel, dictatorial, and repressive governments secretly, and sometimes openly, imprisoned citizens that spoke out against their policies – even governments that voted for the declaration. He read about it all the time. But a standard had been set, which, in the long run, should prevail.

On this November train ride, Peter read that two university students in Portugal had been sentenced to seven years in prison for drinking a toast to liberty in public. *In Portugal?* Not in some

4

uninformed, faraway place, but in Portugal. To use his own words, he felt "sickened and disgusted."

He decided to take action because, he wrote, if "disgust could be united into common action, something effective could be done."

# *From Outrage to Change: The Amnesty International Story*

Peter Benenson consulted friends to help clarify the root cause of his outrage. Then he wrote an article titled "The Forgotten Prisoners." First published in *The Observer* in 1961, the article drew attention to the two students and other "prisoners of conscience," a term he coined for those imprisoned, tortured, or executed because their opinions or beliefs were unacceptable to their governments. The article was picked up by a dozen other newspapers, triggering a write-in campaign that resulted in the release of the Portuguese students. The article also launched an international "Appeal for Amnesty" that grew into Amnesty International.

Since its founding, Amnesty International has carefully thought through its purpose. Early on, Amnesty launched a campaign to end torture around the world, winning the Nobel Peace Prize for its efforts in 1977. The organization helps the families of prisoners of conscience find safe countries in which to live. It campaigns *against* the death penalty, violence to women, arms sales, the use of tazers by police; it campaigns *for* the rights of women, children, refugees, indigenous peoples, as well as prisoners of conscience.

As Amnesty International grew into a global organization, it divided into "sections" that roughly correspond to national offices. Initially, each section was responsible for three prisoners – one in a communist country, one in a capitalist country, and one in a developing country.

At first, Amnesty International used only the power of its members' pens to embarrass abusive governments and corporations. With dedication and persistence, members wrote letters and newspaper articles and circulated reports for publication. Eventually, they added a wide range of non-violent tactics to expose human-rights violations, such as attending trials as observers and holding vigils. They established an annual, international Human Rights Day, December 10, on which they host solemn candle-lighting ceremonies worldwide. Members dance at fundraising events known as Secret Policeman's Balls, promote giant music concerts, circulate global petitions, post blogs – all to call attention to their cause.

Their actions follow a strict moral code. Amnesty International chooses only non-violent methods to make its points and supports only non-violent individuals. The organization refused to support Nelson Mandela, for instance, even though he was a prisoner of conscience, because at the time, Mandela called for the violent overthrow of his South African, apartheid government.

Also, Amnesty does not endorse or criticize any form of government or even the prisoners it works to free. The organization offers no ideological, political, or religious preference – it will challenge any government or corporation on any human-rights abuse. Amnesty impeccably researches every case and saves all files in a library.

National offices do not focus on local abuses. The concern is, when an issue is close to home, members may listen to excuses and let problems slide. The organization accepts no funds from governments or corporations and strictly accounts for all individual donations. These measures reduce the possibility for conflict of interest or corruption within the organization. Amnesty is transparent to its members – democratic, self-governing, and open.

In the fifty years since Peter Benenson published his article, Amnesty has seen the release of about one-third of the prisoners it has supported. There are now 150 sections and 2.2 million members worldwide.

The logo of Amnesty International illustrates its motto: "It is better to light a candle than to curse the darkness."

**STRATEGIES**

# Your Cause, Your Choice

TV talk-show host Phil Donahue interviewed American folk-singer Joan Baez about her volunteer work in support of the Mothers of the Disappeared. Between 1976 and 1983, under military dictatorship in Argentina, up to thirty thousand people disappeared. Some were infants, given to military families to raise as their own. As more people went missing, their mothers and grandmothers strove to find them and to publicize the crime. Amnesty International and other human-rights groups took up the cause, and committed celebrities like Joan Baez brought the issue into the world spotlight.

One woman in the "Phil Donahue Show" audience asked Baez why she didn't support an important *American* problem, such as the war on drugs. Joan asked the questioner if the war on drugs really mattered to her. When the woman said she was very concerned about drugs in America, Joan quietly suggested since *she* was so passionate about it, *she* should put *her* time and effort into that cause. Joan didn't argue which cause mattered most.

Only Joan Baez knows how many times she had been asked that or a similar question. Remarkably, even though she was being asked to justify her support for a cause that meant a lot to her, she kept her cool and answered the question carefully and respectfully, inviting the woman to get involved in what mattered to *her.*

To date, most of the disappeared have never been found, alive or dead. And few of the perpetrators have been brought to justice or made accountable for their crimes. The only redeeming part of this tragic event in history is the ongoing drive and commitment of those who took up the cause of the disappeared.

## SKILLS

# *Walking the Talk: Drawing Your Ethical Self-Portrait*

If a classmate passionately speaks out on the cruel treatment of dogs at a local puppy kennel, but regularly boots his sister's annoying cat out of his room – you might wonder what is going on in his head. Maybe his sister and her friends don't take his puppy talk seriously. Strangely enough, if you point out the double standard, he may be surprised. Often people are blind to how others see their actions. That's why it's a good idea to take a measure of yourself and create your own ethical self-portrait, even if it takes a little time – when you are fed up and eager to confront a wrong. And you may have to confront your dark side too. Don't worry, no one is perfect.

What was it that Peter Benenson found so outrageous about

Portugal imprisoning students for toasting freedom? Stupidity? Cruelty? Hypocrisy?

Amnesty International imposes rules on itself so it does not repeat the behavior it criticizes – even when a cause it has identified is infuriating. The organization takes a collective breath and thinks through its response. As a result, no one can turn on Amnesty and call it hypocritical or cruel or stupid – and be believed.

What outrages you? What behavior is at the root of that? What behavior would you value instead? Answering these questions will help you draw up your ethical stance.

Use the following checklists as a starting point to create your ideal self-portrait. First, tick off what behaviors you despise. Then choose four or five key behaviors you admire to counterbalance what you despise. Don't choose too many – you need to really focus on actions. If what you want is not on the list, add it. Then, practice what you preach, so that you and your cause cannot be dismissed.

You denounce behavior that is

O aggrandizing
O aggressive
O careless
O cruel
O dishonest
O exaggerating
O hypocritical
O insinuating
O intolerant
O judgmental
O lazy
O minimizing

O misleading
O polluting
O racist
O self-righteous
O self-serving
O sneaky
O stereotyping
O stupid
O thoughtless
O violent
O wasteful
O _____

You value behavior that is

O attentive

O careful

O courageous

O creative

O empathetic

O energetic

O enthusiastic

O fair

O faithful

O honest

O honorable

O inclusive

O inspirational

O optimistic

O persevering

O pioneering

O principled

O productive

O reliable

O respectful

O responsible

O selfless

O thoughtful

O truthful

O virtuous

O _____

Now, consider how you might apply your ethical stance. You know which behaviors you dislike and which you admire – how do they apply to your everyday, personal life?

- At home, with your parents and siblings?
- At school, with your teachers and classmates?
- In your neighborhood?
- With your friends?
- With the people in your community?

Look into the cause you are about to embrace. Can you anticipate where you might find your ideal behavior challenged?

- In working with others?
- In trying to raise awareness of the issue beyond your supporters?

- In a power struggle with those who oppose the change you want?

You've taken a few moments – that's probably enough. Don't get tied in knots with self-examination and lose your energy. Go for it!

**TIMELINE** *MILESTONES AND SETBACKS*

# *Human Rights*

The idea that all people share the same basic human rights – no matter who rules the land – has taken centuries to develop. Times of terrible slaughter, mass slavery, genocide, torture, and tyranny have been punctuated by moments of humanity:

**c. 1770 B.C., Iraq:** King Hammurabi cuts his 282 laws of Babylon into a stone tablet, which include the assumption of innocence until proof of guilt and the right to submit evidence. Slavery is acknowledged, however, and people who shelter runaways are sentenced to death.

**539 B.C., Iran:** King Cyrus of Persia issues a code of laws, written on a cylinder, that includes the abolition of slavery and the right of all citizens to worship freely.

**c. 442 B.C., Greece:** Sophocles writes *Antigone*, a play in which the heroine disobeys the king's command and buries her dead brother, claiming she follows a law higher than the king's.

**c. 260 B.C., India:** Ashoka the Great declares that condemned prisoners will not be executed immediately, but will have three days for appeal. He also gives prisoners the right to go outside one day a year.

**71 B.C., Italy:** Spartacus, the leader of a slave rebellion against the Roman Republic, dies, and his uprising fails. More than one-quarter of all the people in Italy are Roman slaves with no rights.

**A.D. 534, Turkey:** Emperor Justinian prepares a codebook of Roman law, which declares the existence of a law above communities that is natural, eternal, and unchangeable and that applies equally to all nations and all peoples.

**A.D. 1215, England:** The barons force King John to sign the Magna Carta, which establishes their right to appeal unlawful imprisonment (habeas corpus), own and inherit property, have equality before the law and a legal system free from bribery.

**A.D. 1478, Spain:** King Ferdinand II and Queen Isabella I, with the support of the Pope, establish the Inquisition, which, over time, persecutes, exiles, imprisons, tortures, and/or executes thousands of Jews, Muslims, and Christians said to undermine the Catholic faith.

**A.D. 1776, United States:** Thomas Jefferson composes the Declaration of Independence, asserting that all men are created equal and share inalienable rights, including life, liberty, and the pursuit of happiness.

**A.D. 1789, France:** The National Assembly approves the Declaration of the Rights of Man, which asserts the natural rights of all men to liberty, property, security, and resistance to oppression. Citizens may speak, write, and publish with freedom as long as no other citizen is hurt.

**A.D. 1864, Switzerland:** The Geneva Convention sets international humanitarian standards for non-combatants and prisoners of war.

**A.D. 1933, Germany:** The Nazi Regime opens its first concentration camp, with two hundred inmates considered to be dangerous Communists. Eventually, Nazi camps hold, torture, and/or kill their political opponents, a category of people that comes to also include journalists, intellectuals, homosexuals, Catholic priests, people with disabilities, Roma and Polish people, and, ultimately, millions of Jews.

**A.D. 1937, Russia:** Joseph Stalin begins the Great Purge, in which hundreds of thousands of people are arrested for "counterrevolutionary activities" and sent to prison labor camps, mostly in remote areas of Siberia. Over the next two years, tens of thousands of these prisoners are executed for "continuing anti-Soviet activity in imprisonment."

**A.D. 1948, United States:** Members of the newly formed United Nations unanimously pass the Universal Declaration of Human Rights. The Soviet Bloc, apartheid South Africa, and Saudi Arabia abstain.

**A.D. 1996, Afghanistan:** Hard-line Taliban rulers deny all women basic human rights, including access to education and jobs. After the fall of the Taliban in 2001, a new constitution recognizes women's rights, but insurgent warlords continue to target women who try to go to school, work, run for office, or vote.

**A.D. 1997, Norway:** Human Rights Watch, an organization that publicizes oppression and oppressors, shares the Nobel Peace Prize for its part in the International Campaign to Ban Landmines.

**A.D. 2002, Netherlands:** Sixty countries set up the International Criminal Court, governed by the Rome Statute, to bring those who commit genocide, crimes against humanity, and war crimes to justice.

**A.D. 2008, China:** Although the constitution guarantees freedom of speech, instant message software is modified to filter words deemed "sensitive" by the authorities. Critics claim key words such as "Tibet" and "democracy" are censored on Internet search engines.

**A.D. 2009, Myanmar:** Prisoner of conscience for fourteen of the last twenty years, Aung San Suu Kyi – once prime minister-elect and later opposition leader – is sentenced to a further eighteen months of house arrest after an American swims across a lake, lands at her door, and she lets him in.

# WHAT'S WRONG?

At first, Ann hardly noticed the green slime in the lake. But then, one summer, she waded out to her favorite diving rock and slipped climbing up the side.

Next summer, soft fingers of bright green algae appeared on the bottom of the boat dock and up the ladder to the waterline. A couple of summers later, the pebbles in the water along the beach lost their shine, all covered in dull green and brown goo. Walking got so hard, Ann wore swim shoes with extra grip over her bare feet.

On the other side of the dock from the swimming area was a shallow bay filled with reeds and dragonflies. At dusk, Ann liked to paddle a boat there and watch for the resident heron, frogs, and minnows. But then the water turned cloudy, and it was harder to see the underwater creatures. Finally, a summer came when dozens of minnows floated belly-up between the reeds. Their rotting bodies stank, and everyone could smell them up in the cabin.

Ann was sure the slime invasion and the dead fish came from

pollution dumped by some nasty pulp mill or mining operation that fed into the lake.

That summer, a university student came to the back door of the cabin with a different story. He said the slime and the dead fish were caused by cottagers – not necessarily by any one family, but by all the people who lived around the lake. Poorly maintained septic tanks drained human sewage, filled with phosphates, into the lake, resulting in the overgrowth of algae and the death of fish. Household detergents flushed into the lake also increased phosphate levels. The student invited Ann to a meeting of everyone who vacationed by the lake in summer. And he left a pamphlet explaining the problem and offering ways individuals could change their habits to bring back the beautiful lake they loved. And that's how Ann Love got involved with Pollution Probe.

Today, the heron, frogs, and minnows are back in Ann's shallow bay, and the reed stems are almost free of algae. At dusk on summer evenings, Ann likes to paddle there again.

**STORY**

# DO IT! The Founding of Pollution Probe

In the mid-1960s, students might have heard the word "environment" in spelling bees because it was uncommon and frequently misspelled. The word "ecology" was used by academics in universities. Environmental studies did not exist in school curriculums. Biology, chemistry, law, history, language, and politics were studied separately in schools – to consider them together was thought to diminish the individual subjects.

There were no departments or ministries of the environment at any level of government. There were no environmental assessments nor environmental impact statements. Conservation groups existed, but mostly connected with sportfishing, hunting, and bird-watching. There were subdepartments of government that managed air and water quality.

A University of Toronto professor, Dr. Donald Chant, who specialized in the study of mites, became head of the Department of Zoology. In 1969, he, his colleagues, and students felt increasingly frustrated that their reports and studies on toxicology and pollution, on the declines in populations of native fish and waterbirds, on the increase in populations of nonnative species, and on asthma and allergies in humans were all collecting dust on a shelf. So Dr. Chant gathered together a group of political science, law, history, business, philosophy, language, as well as science students to get the message out. They called themselves Pollution Probe at the University of Toronto.

Under the motto DO IT! Pollution Probe determined to move environmental issues to the top of political and corporate agendas, to put environmental studies into school curriculums, and to raise public awareness of environmental pollution. One of Pollution Probe's first big campaigns was directed at phosphate pollution.

Scientists at the university had been tracking the unchecked growth of plant life, particularly algae, in the Great Lakes watershed. In many places, the underwater rock was unnaturally slimy. Big blooms of algae caught onto stems of native plants, such as water lilies, and ballooned through bays. This blocked out the sun, and the underwater habitat changed. When the algae died, their decomposition used up oxygen in the water. Fish species died in great numbers. The scientists said the cause was phosphates pouring into the lakes in human sewage, fertilizer, manure

17

runoff from farm fields, and in an additive in household detergents that helped make whites whiter. In 1965, a Canada-United States intergovernmental commission recommended both countries cut back on phosphate discharges into the Great Lakes to halt growing dead zones on the bottom of Lake Erie. But the machinery of change in government was glacial. And there were no freedom-of-information laws yet, so consumers didn't know the phosphate content of household detergents.

Pollution Probers, led by science graduate and activist Brian Kelly, decided the public had the right to know the phosphate levels in household products. Brian and his wife, Ruth, spent much of their Christmas holidays in 1969 testing about one hundred brands of laundry and dish detergents for phosphate levels. They came up with a list, which they read aloud on an investigative television show the following February, then issued a press release the next day. Many newspapers and magazines published the list – it was a media hit.

As well as the list, Pollution Probers reduced the long and complicated chemical pollution story into accurate but short briefs, pamphlets, articles, press releases, advertisements, and talks. They went to the newspapers, radio and TV, offices, boardrooms, ratepayer associations, and people's doors, asking everyone to pressure the government to make stiffer regulations for municipal sewage treatment and septic tanks in cottage country. They challenged the detergent manufacturers to change their additives and asked people to switch to a brand with lower phosphate levels. At the time, there was only one common brand of laundry detergent that did not contain phosphates; of course, old-fashioned laundry soap flakes contained no phosphates and were acceptable.

Many people were enthusiastic when they understood the interconnections between sewage, detergent, and their drinking water.

Offering ways they could actually help in their everyday lives made the prospect attractive to both the media and consumers. But the detergent manufacturers were furious: they insisted they needed more proof, questioning the information and experience of university students. Pollution Probe retorted that they didn't need to spend any more time proving anything. They said it's not up to the public to prove that a product is harming the environment; it's up to the manufacturer to prove to the public that it's *not*. That was an amazingly radical idea – one that has finally been upheld, thirty-five years later, by the Supreme Court of Canada. Under public pressure, the detergent companies changed their products. And today, one of the companies runs a foundation that gives money to environmental education.

Pollution Probers were careful to be accurate with their facts, but also to not get trapped in endless technical investigations or arguing about definitions. They put their efforts into finding ways to get the message out and to empowering ordinary people to be part of the solution.

As a result of the efforts of Pollution Probe and others, today we have environmental curriculums in schools, assessments, departments in governments, vice presidents in large corporations, as well as more open access to information. But we still have other environmental issues to tackle and need to come up with fresh tactics to make citizens aware and ready to DO IT!

# Comebacks to Put-Downs

In his book *Rules for Radicals*, author Saul Alinsky advises that ridicule is the most potent, non-violent weapon available. People who are broadsided with ridicule start to seethe inside. In fact, they usually splutter so badly, they prove the point of their attacker.

You may decide to use ridicule as a tactic, or you may choose to avoid put-downs. Whatever you decide, it's a good idea to pre-plan your reaction if *someone ridicules you*. As a change-maker, you and your ideas may be threatening. You could find yourself in a power struggle with those who think they will lose money, influence, their livelihood, or even their comfort zone with any change in the status quo. Fighting from a corner, these people may lash out, ridiculing you personally.

You will feel the sting of ridicule before you know what's happening. It often strikes hardest through tone of voice. You feel totally disrespected and may react before thinking. And then you've had it – the spluttering begins. The best move is to pause and refocus on the facts, on what is wrong.

Idealistic young people are often attacked for their presumed lack of research, knowledge, and/or experience. Ever hear these comments? Don't forget to add a nasty tone of voice:

*"Why should anyone believe someone like you? What do you know about this anyway?"*

*"If you had any experience, you'd know what you're suggesting is ridiculous."*

*"If you understood the subject, you wouldn't be asking those questions."*

Plan your response. Deflect the ridicule. Use a neutral voice and avoid lashing back with more ridicule – if you hope to get anything accomplished quickly:

*"This is not about me, it's about _____ [the facts]."*
*"Ridiculing my experience doesn't change the fact that something is wrong and has to be addressed."*
*"I appreciate the scope of the problem and want to explore solutions with you."*
*"Your response shows no respect for me, my ideas, or my colleagues."*

Political debates are full of sharp ridicule and great comeback lines. Check out videos, blogs, and news reports of presidential and party-leader debates for some fabulous examples.

# The Long and the Short of It: Writing a Brief

You've identified a situation that has to change – including what's wrong. First, find out all you possibly can about it. Then, choose a way to present your case as clearly, as persuasively, and as concisely as possible. Write it down in a well-crafted brief. Even if it is never published and you end up giving interviews on TV and radio shows instead, having composed a thoughtful, well-written brief is excellent preparation.

## Research: The Long of It

Take time on the research. You want to investigate and understand all sides of the issue so you can talk about it without stumbling.

Keep detailed notes and sort your points into categories. Speak to friends about what you're learning and, from their response, see what you need to delve into more deeply to make a stronger case. Look for background stories that enhance your knowledge of the situation – even if you never use that information again. Above all, think what you can provide as *new* information because that will make your brief newsworthy.

### Creating a Brief: The Short of It

When you have the subject down cold, tap into your gut feelings. What is it that makes your concern so important? Can you summarize your case in one or two sentences? If so, you are ready to write a brief.

Consider your audience. Who needs to hear your concerns – other kids, government officials, neighbors? What do they need to know? What don't they care about? And remember, people are busy . . . they will not read something long-winded, unfocused, or rambling. Even if it matters, they won't take the time.

Decide which communication method will best reach the people who can make your change happen. Are you trying to convince a person or group directly, or are you trying to broadcast your case to a larger community so that many people put pressure on that person or group? Decide your medium: a newspaper article, a letter to the editor, a flyer in the mailbox, a posting on a blog, or a remark on a Facebook wall?

Keep your audience in mind, and write your argument persuasively. If writing for a newspaper, create a document on one page that the editor can "cut and paste," using your exact words. If writing for the Internet, keep your information punchy and short enough to fit on one screen. Are there any illustrations or photos that will add to your case?

Don't forget:

- Compose a strong headline. Your headline should include what is *new* to the story you are telling.
- In your introductory paragraph, continue the drama of the headline. Keep it short – three sentences long. Be sure to answer who, what, where, when, why, and how (five *w*'s and a *h*).
- In the middle of your brief – use several paragraphs – be crisp in your choice of language, and use lots of action words. If possible, include a story or anecdote – people remember stories. And give your readers something they can do about the problem so they can do it!
- At the end, include where to go for more information and how you can be contacted by E-mail (do not include your street address or home phone number).
- Be sure the date is somewhere on the brief.
- Format with wide margins, double spacing, and a standard, easy-to-read font.
- Provide high-resolution visuals, with captions no longer than seven words. Include photo credits.

**TIMELINE** **MILESTONES AND SETBACKS**

# *Air and Water Pollution*

Humankind has battled air and water pollution for hundreds of years. Some of the great pollution disasters and victories reverberate today:

**c. 50 B.C., Spain:** Toxic smoke from the Rio Tinto lead mine travels as far as Greenland, where it is trapped in ice and detected in glacier core samples two thousand years later.

**A.D. 1157, England:** Queen Eleanor of Aquitaine flees Tutbury Castle, where air pollution from unendurable, dense wood smoke hurts her lungs.

**A.D. 1711, Ireland:** Jonathan Swift describes the London gutters as full of "sweepings from butchers' stalls, dung, guts, blood, drowned puppies, stinking sprats . . ."

**A.D. 1849, United States:** New Yorkers call for improved sewers and the expulsion of pigs from city streets when five thousand poor people die of cholera.

**A.D. 1873, England:** Approximately one thousand people die of killer smog from coal fires in London, famous for its smoky, dirty skies and nights of greasy fog.

**A.D. 1921, United States:** Leaded gasoline goes on sale without safety tests, and two years later, five refinery workers become "violently insane" and die. The sale of leaded gasoline is finally phased out in 1976 for health and safety reasons.

**c. A.D. 1929, United States:** PCBs and CFCs are introduced into manufacturing; both prove to be so hazardous and lingering in the environment that production of PCBs is banned in 1976 and CFCs in 1978.

**A.D. 1950, India:** The new constitution declares the right of all citizens to fresh air and sweet water as part of the right to life and personal liberty.

**A.D. 1956, Japan:** Dozens die and hundreds are disabled from the consumption of fish contaminated by mercury discharged into the water of Minamata Bay. Over time, thousands of newborns suffer brain damage and birth defects because their mothers ate contaminated fish.

**A.D. 1962, United States:** Rachel Carson publishes *Silent*

*Spring* and draws attention to the harmful environmental effects of pesticides, DDT in particular.

**A.D. 1969, United States:** Oil and debris on the Cuyahoga River catch fire; some flames reach five stories high above the water.

**A.D. 1978, United States:** Governments evacuate hundreds of families from a subdivision in Niagara Falls, New York, constructed on toxic waste, used to fill in an old man-made waterway called the Love Canal.

**A.D. 1981, Canada:** Environmentalists form the Canadian Coalition on Acid Rain to lobby the governments of the United States and Canada to legislate restrictions on acid-rain-producing emissions. They disband in 1990, after the passage of the Clean Air Act in the United States.

**A.D. 1984, India:** In Bhopal, more than two thousand people die overnight, thousands more over the following years, and tens of thousands suffer health problems after a Union Carbide pesticide plant releases lethal gas into the air. Toxic chemicals abandoned at the site continue to pollute the groundwater to this day.

**A.D. 1986, Ukraine:** The Chernobyl nuclear reactor explodes, killing fifty-six people immediately and more than four thousand over time from radiation poisoning.

**A.D. 1988, Indian Ocean:** After dumping four thousand tons of toxic incinerator ashes from Philadelphia on a beach in Haiti, the cargo vessel *Khian Sea* illegally dumps the remaining ten thousand tons of waste in the Atlantic and Indian oceans.

**A.D. 1991, Kuwait:** At the end of the First Gulf War, the retreating Iraqi army sets fire to hundreds of oil wells and creates the largest oil spill ever.

**A.D. 1995, Nigeria:** The government executes author Ken Saro-Wiwa, whose last words were "Lord, take my soul, but the struggle continues." Saro-Wiwa formed the Movement for the Survival of the Ogoni People to protest pollution of the Niger River Delta by oil companies, Shell Oil in particular.

**A.D. 2000, Canada:** Heavy rain washes E. coli from manure on farm fields into a well providing drinking water to residents of Walkerton, Ontario, leaving seven people dead and over 2,300 seriously ill.

**A.D. 2002, United States:** A jury convicts the Monsanto Company on many counts, including "outrage" – a legal term meaning "conduct atrocious and utterly intolerable in civilized society" – for polluting Anniston, Alabama, with tons of PCBs.

**A.D. 2005, China:** An explosion at a Jilin Petrochemical plant releases one hundred tons of toxic chemicals and pollutes the drinking water of millions of people in China and Russia. Official attempts to keep the release secret result in widespread protests.

**A.D. 2008, Denmark:** The international Blue Flag program, run by Denmark's Foundation for Environmental Education, awards 2,585 beaches in thirty-one countries the right to fly their eco-label flag because the beaches all meet strict criteria for water quality, environmental management, and safety.

**A.D. 2010, Gulf of Mexico:** A catastrophic explosion on an offshore drilling rig leaves oil gushing from the seafloor. A giant oil slick, growing uncontrollably and blown by strong winds, fouls beaches and wetlands, killing millions of plants, birds, fish, turtles and mammals. To date, it is the worst environmental disaster in U.S. history.

# GREAT MINDS
# THINK ALIKE

**P**icture this scenario. The year is 1999, and the premier of Ontario is working at his office desk. A harried assistant rushes into the room with a sheaf of E-mails from different interest groups. All bristle with urgency and demand decisions on the future of the great northern forest. The premier scans the subject lines:

"A Healthy Forest is a Timber-Managed Forest!" declares an E-mail from a logger's union.

"Ban All Cutting in Ancient Forests!" a wilderness advocate's words cry out.

"The Gifts of Nature are for the Benefit of People," a mining company's E-mail begins.

"Development Threatens Woodland Caribou," a prominent wildlife conservationist asserts.

"Protect Duck Breeding Habitat," a group of wetland advocates demands.

"Aboriginal Rights on All Traditional Lands," a First Nation's subject line states.

"Chainsaws Silence Birdsong!" a bird-watcher warns.

The interest groups don't seem to agree on what's wrong. The premier has to prioritize. Whatever the government decides, a large group with a stake in the northern forest will be angry.

Of course, no such cluster of E-mails was sent in 1999, but the government did receive conflicting messages and appeals from important groups with vested interests in the forest.

Now, fast-forward ten years – and this really happened.

The premier takes a microphone and announces to the media a plan for the future of the northern forest that includes the protection of an area greater than the size of Idaho or Kansas. Behind him, on the platform, stand members of the interest groups. Some are nodding, some smile broadly.

*What changed?* The stakeholders got together and forged a partnership. They agreed on what was wrong and came up with a plan for the future. Together, they spoke with such a powerful voice, they could not be ignored.

**STORY**

# Minding Both the Forest and the Trees: The Boreal Partnership

At the turn of the millennium, the Pew Charitable Trusts of Philadelphia, an American non-profit organization, resolved to do as much as it could to protect Canada's northern boreal forest before it was too late. The organization hired staff to set up the Canadian Boreal Initiative and partner with the First Nations, logging companies, the mining industry, and conservation groups that shared a stake in the forest.

The Canadian boreal forest holds one-quarter of Earth's original forests. While we humans inhale oxygen and exhale carbon dioxide, forests do the reverse – they breathe out oxygen and breathe in carbon dioxide. The vast boreal ecosystem provides us with fresh clean air and, in the same breath, absorbs our waste carbon dioxide. The boreal forest is so vast, it moderates climate change by also storing some of the carbon dioxide contaminating our air from the burning of fossil fuels.

But it's not only about clean air and a stable climate. The Canadian boreal forest is the source of much of the freshwater on Earth, with over 1.5 million lakes and sprawling river systems. Uncountable wetlands naturally filter and purify that water.

Meanwhile, the Canadian boreal forest is a nursery for billions of insects and birds; prime habitat for large populations of wolves, bears, moose, and caribou; and a place to work and call home for hundreds of thousands of people.

In 2003, the Canadian Boreal Initiative felt it had ten years to make an impact before logging, mining, and development cut too deeply into the forest for Nature to thrive. Protecting the vastness of the ecosystem and the sheer number of trees would contribute vital air, water, and climate services to everyone on Earth.

With a small staff, the Canadian Boreal Initiative brought together a committee to prepare a model plan for the future of the boreal forest. Members called their plan a framework, determining who would likely sign on as partners and who wouldn't. They knew the broader their reach, the more powerful their voice would be; so they planned to negotiate, cultivate, and minimize any opposition by agreeing to modify aspects of the framework.

After negotiation, First Nations peoples signed on, including the Innu of Labrador, the Poplar River First Nation of Manitoba, the Treaty 8 First Nations of Alberta, the Kaska Nation of British Columbia and Yukon, and the Dehcho First Nations of northern Canada. Major logging companies – Domtar, Al-Pac, and Tembec – got involved, as did the big global energy companies Suncor and Nexen. Financial and marketing companies – such as Domini, Ethical Funds, and ForestEthics – participated. And Ducks Unlimited, World Wildlife Fund, and the Nature Conservancy were some of the conservation groups in on the action.

These partners agreed to implement the framework in their different work worlds. Together, they called for the complete protection of half of Canada's boreal forest and sustainable development for the other half. The strictly protected half was to be interconnected so the scope and integrity of the original forest remained.

Coming up with this final framework took serious consideration and compromise. On topics outside the issue at hand, some groups disagreed strongly with each other. For instance, perhaps they didn't agree on the seriousness of climate change or the safety of nuclear energy. Or if they did agree, some may not have been comfortable with the methods and tactics others suggested to effect change. And each partner had to take the details of the agreement back to their larger organization for approval while the corporations had to be sure the outcome would still provide profit to their shareholders. Perhaps the agreement even affected their business plans. The non-profit conservation groups had to share credit with each other for any victories and sort out how that would affect donations to their other causes. First Nations had to make sure the framework fit into their land claims and the future they hoped for their people.

Each member of the partnership also brought something to the table, with contacts and skills to share. For example, some were able to broker meetings with senior government officials more easily than others. And money from the Canadian Boreal Initiative supported the travel, research, and planning needed to come up with the agreement.

Governments listen when so many important stakeholders make a commitment. Within five years of the initial members formally signing the framework, the federal government agreed to set aside huge tracts of forest in the Northwest Territories – one the size of Prince Edward Island. The Ontario government announced plans to protect over 22 million hectares (about 54 million acres) of the forest under the guidelines of the framework. And the Quebec government pledged to set aside fifty percent of the boreal forest in that province from any industrial development.

The goals of the framework are not yet fulfilled, but the partners are well on their way to success.

**STRATEGIES**

# Walking a Mile in Your Opponent's Shoes

Even in his student days, Monte Hummel showed an uncanny ability to identify and understand many different points of view. A fierce debater through school who enjoyed playing devil's advocate, he turned his talents to wildlife conservation. Now he is president emeritus of World Wildlife Fund (WWF) Canada, who, over forty years, has won many to his cause – including the presidents of large companies. Among the most recent is a partnership he forged with the chief executive of De Beers Canada, which produces about forty percent of the world's supply of rough diamonds.

De Beers has a big interest in diamonds under the permafrost in the barren lands west of Hudson's Bay, in northern Canada. Hummel and WWF Canada have concerns for the barren lands' habitat, in particular, its signature species, the barren-ground caribou.

The barren lands are an immense "treeless" wilderness that comprises most of mainland Nunavut, stretching north from the remote regions of Manitoba and Saskatchewan right up to the Arctic Ocean. Not literally treeless, the barren lands are forested with birch and willows that usually grow only as tall as your thumb. Traditional hunting ground to both the Inuit and Dene, the barren lands are home to huge numbers of ducks, geese, and shorebirds as well as muskoxen, wolves, foxes, grizzly bears, and caribou. Because the barren lands are so rich in wildlife, areas in the central Arctic have been set aside as a migratory bird sanctuary, a wildlife sanctuary, and even a proposed national park. These areas interconnect to create a wildlife-safe corridor from Great Slave Lake to the Arctic Ocean . . . except for one critical break, which happens to be the calving grounds of the Beverly barren-ground caribou herd.

In 2000, Hummel set out to find a way to protect these calving grounds from industrial development. As there are no trees big enough to log on the barren lands, development means mining. He discovered that the calving grounds had already been staked by diamond and uranium prospectors. So, over the next few years, he met with communities in the area and found strong local support and leadership for more protection. But try as he might, he did not find willingness in all the necessary, but far-away government capitals to secure the calving grounds. So, he thought, if the biggest mining company agreed not to operate in the calving grounds, that would set an example for others to follow.

Hummel found out all he could about De Beers – the company leaders, the diamond exploration, and the mining. And he double-checked his facts on the caribou. He knew, when he sat down at the table with the head and senior executives, that his information had to be as good as or better than theirs. Then he put his mind to what De Beers would think about his protection plan and how it could benefit the company.

When Hummel met with the president of De Beers, he was ready. He'd even found out the man loved good coffee, so he came with a WWF panda coffee mug as a gift for him to drink from while Hummel drank his coffee from a De Beers cup! He knew the man was intelligent and thoughtful as well as powerful. When Hummel goes into such meetings, he assumes the company head is ready for constructive discussion. He doesn't think, "I'm about to face a greedy, stupid, unpleasant person," because people who run giant corporations rarely are. Both his research and experience have told him that.

Hummel talked about how a commitment to stay out of caribou calving areas would be an advantage to De Beers. He began by saying "It seems to me that . . ." and ended with "Have I got that right?" He doesn't tell any president how to run his company – no one likes to hear the words "You should. . . ." Hummel listed what he thought would be the many benefits to De Beers: the local communities through whom the company ships goods and finds workers all wanted the calving areas protected; the news media would pounce on such a dramatic decision and flood De Beers with good public relations, especially in the North, where it operated; De Beers would be praised as an environmental leader in the mining industry; areas in the barren lands *outside* protected areas would likely be open for sustainable development; and more. . . .

Of course, the president of De Beers had to step back and consider what Hummel was proposing. But, on October 24, 2008, he wrote a letter on De Beers' letterhead committing the company to not conduct activities in *any* barren-ground caribou calving area.

Success – and more work. Hummel uses the De Beers' leadership to leverage governments and companies who haven't committed to protecting caribou calving grounds. When confronted with opposition, he applies his method:

- *Do your homework.* Conduct the best research.
- *Look for a win/win solution.* Think through how a commitment to conservation will benefit the developer and local communities.
- *Respect the opposition.* Believe the senior officials will be thoughtful, concerned, good people.
- *Listen and learn.* Offer suggestions starting with "It seems to me that . . ." and ending with "Have I got that right?"
- *Build on success.* Use any success to lever a further step in the right conservation direction.

**SKILLS**

# Two Heads Are Better than One: Running a Good Meeting

Once you identify your supporters and partners, you may want to call a meeting so you can involve them in action. A well-run meeting offers a place to talk through a subject, learn different aspects of it, and develop an action plan. A poorly run meeting can poison a partnership and sap energy from supporters.

Perhaps you learn that the swimming pool in your local high school will be closed to save money. You know lots of kids who use the pool and think, working together, you could possibly come up with a way to stop the closure.

Here are the things to consider to run a successful meeting:

## 1. The Purpose

Set your goals. If a meeting runs with a tight focus, it will be shorter, pertinent, and motivating.

- Write down, in one or two sentences, the reason for the meeting. Refer to it if people stray off topic.

## 2. The Participants

People will attend your meeting if they believe you value their ideas. They will come to your next meeting if they feel they made a contribution at the first one, their time was respected, and the meeting met its goal.

- Draw up a list of all potential attendees and notify them of the meeting's purpose.
- Canvass them to find a convenient place and time to meet. Inform them of the chosen time and place as soon as possible.

## 3. The Location

Find a place with comfortable seating and arrange it so each participant feels a valued part of the group.

- A circle arrangement for a small or midsized group is inclusive and welcoming.
- Position the chairperson at a focal point in the circle.

- If there are too many people to form a circle, place the chairs in rows. Offset the chairs so everyone can see and make eye contact.

## 4. The Agenda

Although it seems formal, an agenda keeps the meeting on topic, on time, and the action focused.

- The chair or caller of the meeting prepares the agenda and delivers it to the participants several days in advance. This gives them time to collect their thoughts.
- The task at hand can be separated into sections for discussion. For instance, an agenda could include a short list of options for action – a telephone campaign, a rally, a petition, or other ways to get the word out. If your group already knows you are planning a rally, your agenda might list items such as place, time, placards, brochures, information table, press release, crowd control, notification of authorities, and so on.
- At the beginning of the meeting, the chair asks participants if they have anything to add to the agenda.

## 5. The Vote

Before the first vote, everyone needs to agree on how decisions will be made. They are usually decided by consensus.

- After discussion, a motion (or statement) is formulated.
- The motion is read, and participants express their agreement by a show of hands.
- If no participants are against it, the action moves forward. If some are, discuss it until you have an agreement for action. If necessary, you can always call for a formal vote.

## 6. The Roles

- Chairperson – The chair's job is to ensure the meeting starts and ends promptly, one person speaks at a time, each participant gets a reasonable say, the meeting stays on topic, new ideas are encouraged, and discussions end with a fair vote. The chair states what is on the table and what is to be decided before the vote. He or she summarizes what action must be taken if consensus is reached.

   If you have strong views, want to present them, and hope to persuade others to see it your way, you should not be the chair. A good chair is a facilitator, not a persuader or boss.

- Note-Taker – The secretary or note-taker of the meeting does not write down all that is said, but records who attends, which decisions are made, and which actions will be taken forward. If a record of the proceedings is required, the note-taker will prepare a brief summary called minutes.

## 7. A Positive Contribution

You don't have to be the chair to help a meeting work. You set a healthy tone when you listen carefully, stay on topic, keep it short, and acknowledge other people's ideas. You may be the one who can lighten tension with humor, know the right question to ask, see a compromise, clarify a sticky point, or envision the road ahead. When a meeting works and a team forms around an issue that matters to you, you win.

Let's say your group decides to circulate a petition. After several follow-up meetings, in person or by E-mail, you settle on the wording and how you will gather signatures. Eventually, you deliver the petition signed by 250 people to the school board or local town council. Then, you are invited to attend one of their formal meetings. What should you expect?

1. Organizations that run regular meetings post agendas that include date and time of the meeting, past minutes, old business, new business, etc. Your school board or town council may have a long agenda, and the meeting could take several hours. Portions of the meeting will likely be held "in camera" – or behind closed doors. Ask where you are on the agenda, so you can arrive at the proper time.

2. Established organizations follow clear rules about what constitutes a meeting, what size majority is needed to pass a motion, who can vote, and so on. You can brush up on all the rules in *Robert's Rules of Order*, available in your library or on their official website. Or you can attend the formal meeting, watch, and learn. If you are not given a chance to speak when your petition is considered, you may be asked to stand up so people can see you. If there is time, you will be asked to say a few words, so go prepared. In presenting your issue, clearly read out loud the wording on the petition and note the number of signatures. Then thank the participants for considering your group's concern.

3. Stay until the participants have decided what to do with your concern and have moved on to another item of business. They may come up with a motion to support the pool staying open and call a vote. More likely, they will decide to send your request to a committee or to paid staff for review. Note where it goes so that you can follow up. If you must leave the meeting, the note-taker will record the status of your request in the minutes, and you should be able to access that information later on.

# Forest Stewardship

People have both valued and plundered forests for thousands of years. Our relationship with this amazing habitat has had some remarkable high- and lowlights:

*c. 8000 B.C., Planet Earth:* About 62 million square km (24 million sq. mi.) are cloaked in undisturbed, natural forest.

*c. 2700 B.C., Iraq:* Gilgamesh defies the gods and cuts a stand of great cedar trees. The rulers of Ur pass laws to protect the remaining forest.

*c. 1300 B.C., Greece:* Priests and priestesses interpret the rustlings of oak and beech leaves in the sacred grove at Dodona to advise and answer petitioners.

*c. 55 B.C., France:* Julius Caesar describes the size of the ancient forests of Gaul as sixty days journey long and nine days journey wide.

*c. A.D. 800, China:* Rulers of the Tang Dynasty order the cutting of the Loyang forest for firewood and to make ink from the black carbon residue.

*A.D. 1666, Japan:* The shogun orders the planting of tree seedlings to offset the side effects of deforestation – soil erosion, silting of streams, and flooding.

*A.D. 1778, India:* In an attempt to stop Jodhpur state officials from cutting down sacred khejri trees, Bishnoi villagers hug the tree trunks. The officials ax 363 villagers to death as the trees are cut down.

*A.D. 1845, United States:* Johnny Appleseed (John Chapman) dies after fifty years of planting apple trees across Indiana and Ohio.

**A.D. 1852, United States:** People are outraged when a giant sequoia (bald cypress) tree in California called Mother of the Forest is cut down for display in sideshows.

**A.D. 1872, United States:** The *Nebraska City News* proposes a national Arbor Day.

**A.D. 1976, Brazil:** Rubber tappers led by Chico Mendez form a human chain to stop loggers from cutting down giant rubber trees in the Amazon. Mendez is assassinated by ranchers in 1988 for his continued protests against clear-cutting and burning of the tropical rainforest.

**A.D. 1988, Borneo:** The Penan people gain worldwide attention as they blockade logging sites that threaten their traditional forest homelands.

**A.D. 1997, United States:** Julia Butterfly Hill climbs a California redwood tree, living there for two years in protest of old-growth forest logging.

**A.D. 2010, Canada:** Twenty-one forest companies and nine environmental groups call a truce in their logger vs. tree-hugger battle in the boreal forest. Both sides agree to follow a number of responsible logging standards in return for an area being set aside for forest conservation and the protection of the endangered habitat of the woodland caribou.

**A.D. 2010, Planet Earth:** About 33 million square km (13 million sq. mi.) are wooded, but only about 13 million square km (5 million sq. mi.) remain undisturbed, natural forest (www.globalforestwatch.org).

# GOOD PLANS, GOOD LUCK

**H**ave you recently attended a new school? Do you remember feeling nervous? You probably wondered: "Will I know anyone?" "Where are the bathrooms?" "What should I wear?" You may have rehearsed what you'd say in front of the mirror if anyone asked you questions about yourself: "Yeah, I'm new. You? Cool. . . ."

In 1957, nine African-American students had different worries and rehearsed very different scenarios as they prepared to start a new school. They were the first black students to be integrated into the all-white Little Rock Central High School. Handpicked by Daisy Bates, president of the Arkansas state conference of the National Association for the Advancement of Colored People (NAACP), the three boys and six girls were excellent students, known for good behavior. Daisy Bates warned them to practice patience and dignity – the same passive resolve that Martin Luther King Jr. would use in his crusade for civil rights. The Little Rock Nine, as they'd soon be called, needed these attributes and more to enter the building, let alone complete the year.

The United States Supreme Court declared segregated schools unconstitutional in 1954. Little Rock's school board agreed to follow the law and gradually introduce mixed-race classes. But some members of the white community were adamantly against integration. On the first day of school, Orval Faubus, governor of Arkansas and a segregation sympathizer, used National Guardsmen to prevent the nine students from entering the school. Picture the front pages of newspapers across the country and around the world: hundreds of screaming white protestors, parents, students, armed guards – and nine black teens. It took about three weeks, the intervention of President Dwight Eisenhower, and the 101st Airborne Division of the United States Army for the students to actually complete a day of classes.

It was a tumultuous year. All nine later recalled daily taunts, sneers, and being jostled in the hall. Melba Pattillo had acid thrown in her face. Minnijean Brown turned on her tormentors and threw a bowl of chili on a white boy's head. Her punishment was suspension, and she later moved to New York to complete high school. Someone posted a sign that read ONE DOWN, EIGHT TO Go. But at year's end, Ernest Green became the first black student to graduate from Central High.

Governor Faubus canceled high school for the entire city in the fall of 1958. White students attended schools in neighboring counties or went to white-only private schools. This stalling tactic lasted one school year, and, by 1959, Little Rock schools were fully integrated.

The Little Rock Nine, hailed as heroes of the Civil Rights Movement, were honored with the Congressional Gold Medal in 1998. Their attendance at Little Rock Central High School was a positive action in negative times, paving the way for change.

# Actions Speak Louder Than Words: The Rosa Parks Story

Being in the right place at the right time can be as much about luck as careful planning. Before she stepped into the history books, Rosa Parks could be described as ordinary. Her story was similar to thousands of other hardworking Southerners of her day. A granddaughter of slaves, Rosa and her family were of mixed race – African-American and Scotch-Irish. She grew up in a small, rural Alabama community ruled by the Jim Crow laws. These post-Civil-War laws were enforced between 1876 and 1965. Whites and people "of color" were kept apart in all significant aspects of community life. Services and opportunities were called separate but equal – in restaurants, on trains and buses, at offices or public water fountains.

Rosa knew as a schoolgirl that equality was an illusion. She watched white kids ride by in buses as she and her fellow black students walked. In her neighborhood, schools for whites were well staffed, well supplied, and the buildings were properly maintained, unlike the overcrowded and rundown school Rosa attended. But she never challenged the system. In fact, she left school to look after an ailing grandmother and, later, her mother. When she was twenty, Rosa returned to school as a mature student and completed high school.

Rosa's grandfather, like heads of many black families, sat up numerous nights, guarding his home with a loaded shotgun. The Ku Klux Klan, or KKK, was a powerful white-supremacy group that bullied and terrorized blacks and their sympathizers in order to keep their preferred social order. Hooded in white robes, KKK members marched the streets at night, shouting and brandishing flaming torches. Lynching, tarring and feathering, and arson were their trademarks. Rosa Parks remembers her grandfather as calm, but prepared to take on the mob if he needed to protect the family.

At nineteen, Rosa married her sweetheart, a barber named Raymond Parks. Local blacks came to her husband's shop for more than a haircut. By law, American citizens could vote from 1870 onwards, but a pricey poll tax discouraged or denied many. Only nonwhites were required to pass an examination that tested their literacy and understanding of government. Sometimes ridiculous questions were asked, such as "How many hairs are on a hog's back?" As a member of the NAACP, Raymond Parks was low-key, but did his part to advance civil rights by helping blacks register to vote and pay for legal aid.

Marriage put Rosa in contact with her local NAACP, and she became the recording secretary of the Montgomery branch in 1943 – keeping meticulous notes for the next twelve years. She hadn't sought this role, but, instead, fell into it because she was the only woman present at the first meeting she attended. Despite her obvious writing ability, Rosa failed the voting literacy test twice. On the third try, a well-known NAACP black activist, E.D. Nixon, accompanied her. He encouraged Rosa to record her questions and answers so that she could dispute the ruling with the authorities if she failed again. Rosa's persistence paid off: she finally became a registered voter in 1945.

Ten years later, about ninety years after the abolition of slavery, Rosa Parks climbed on board James Blake's Cleveland Street bus – which she had avoided in the recent past. It was at the discretion of drivers to enforce the bus segregation laws. Blacks sat in a designated section at the back of the bus, clearly marked by a moveable sign known as "the board." Nonwhites could sit in the middle section only if no whites required those seats. No black person could sit beside or across the aisle from a white person. Black passengers boarded the bus at the front, paid the driver, immediately exited, and reentered via the back door. Once, Rosa Parks dropped her purse after paying her fare and sat very briefly in a "whites-only" seat while collecting her bag. James Blake was so furious that he drove away as she was walking to the back entrance. She not only lost her fare, she walked home five miles in the rain.

On December 1, 1955, Rosa took her place in the middle section of James Blake's bus, along with several other black people. When a white man boarded and stood in the aisle, unable to find a seat, James Blake stopped the bus and demanded that Rosa, the man beside her, and the two other women seated across the aisle give up their seats so one white man could sit alone. The others meekly got up, moved farther back, and stood quietly. Rosa refused. The driver warned her that he was going to call the police and have her arrested. She told him to do just that.

Both history and urban lore have recorded that Rosa Parks was an older woman, worn down by fatigue and just too tired to comply with the law. In reality, the forty-two-year-old seamstress was no more physically tired than usual. But Rosa was emotionally weary of giving in and being treated as a second-class citizen. She remained composed during her arrest, transport to jail, fingerprinting, and brief stay behind bars. E.D. Nixon, now president of the local chapter of the NAACP, paid her bail and hired a lawyer to represent her in court on December 5th.

Remaining in her seat was a decision Rosa Parks made on the bus at that moment, but it was years in the making. And her action set off a remarkable chain of events that she could never have foreseen. It was time for change.

# *Seize the Moment*

Rosa Parks was not the first black person to test the rules. But she was an instant celebrity, with rock-solid credibility. She was the catalyst that gave the cause of civil rights the golden opportunity it needed to move forward. Behind the scenes, her supporters recognized that the time was now, and they were quick to act.

E.D. Nixon called for a boycott of every Montgomery bus the day of Rosa's trial. He used all his contacts – including asking black community ministers Ralph Abernathy and Martin Luther King Jr. – to spread word of the boycott from their church pulpits on Sunday, December 4th. Jo Ann Robinson, president of the Women's Political Council, distributed flyers asking all black people, young and old, to boycott the buses all day Monday in support of Rosa Parks. Their call for solidarity worked – united they walked while near-empty buses cruised the streets.

Rosa's trial lasted five minutes. She was found guilty and paid a fine of fourteen dollars. If she'd been let off with a warning, or if the charges had been dismissed, the status quo would likely have continued. But those trying to keep society the same actually gave change a blast of fuel. The Montgomery Bus Boycott continued for 381 more days: blacks walked to work or carpooled, while sympathetic taxi drivers charged a fraction of the fare.

Rosa Parks lost her job, and her husband quit his after being harassed for speaking her name. The KKK firebombed the King, Abernathy, and Nixon homes, and the Parks received death threats. Finally, on December 21, 1956, the United States Supreme Court ruled that bus segregation was illegal.

Rosa Parks turned out to be the right person in the right place at the right time. Most importantly, key players – such as Martin Luther King Jr., Ralph Abernathy, and E.D. Nixon – supported her. They certainly took care of the "who" in who, what, when, why, and where! And luck played its part in aligning the stars, shooting Rosa Parks into the spotlight.

Rosa Parks died in 2005, but imagine how she'd have felt in 2009, when an African-American was elected to the White House. She'd probably be embarrassed by the attention, but she has been given some credit for making this dream come true. A text message received by Khari Mosley, Democratic party chairman for Pittsburgh's 22nd Ward, when Barack Obama was elected president, read "*Rosa sat so Martin could walk; Martin walked so Obama could run; Obama runs so our children can fly!*"

SKILLS

# *Preparing to Face the Media*

You get a message requesting an interview for the local paper. The reporter has heard you're doing terrific work, changing your world. Your heart's pounding and your face flushes with excitement. Yikes! What do you do?

Now that you have her attention, research the writing style of this journalist. Thousands of news stories – whimsical, wrenching, informative, captivating, or horrific – circulate on a daily basis. From these, a few great/pivotal moments are kept alive by photos, video, and commentary. Will you have fifteen minutes of fame or be remembered forever? Everything could hinge on how well you prepare for your media interview.

- What kind of stories does your journalist report?
- What are the headlines of the paper she works for like? Are

they clear? Sensational? Matter-of-fact?

- Is her writing balanced, sympathetic, and insightful or skewed, critical, and cynical?
- Does she use full quotes or chopped-up excerpts?
- Does she seem to have it in for a segment of society?
- Do you suspect a hidden agenda?
- Will her article reach the right people to further your cause?

## Plan One Point, or Three

"I have a nightmare. . . ." If these were the first four words out of Martin Luther King Jr.'s mouth, instead of the iconic "I have a dream," would we still remember him? Be positive when talking to a reporter. Before the interview starts, anticipate the questions and prepare your answers and strategies. It is important to get your message out!

- What is your ultimate goal?
  Write it down. You want to change _____ about your world.
- What have you done to date?
  Prepare a timeline of your accomplishments so far and keep it at your fingertips. If you're nervous during the interview, you can always ground yourself by glancing at these notes.
- What are your proudest moments?
  Toot your horn – just not too loudly. This is your chance to promote yourself and your cause.
- What is your action plan?
  Write a clear, step-by-step action plan for your cause. Focus on what you want to achieve, not on others' failings.
- How can the media help your cause move forward?
  List your priorities: Public Awareness? Donations? Volunteers?
- What is the one essential point you need to make?

If the interviewer is not asking the right questions, get your point across by saying, "I think you are asking me . . ." and then fill in what you really need to say.

- What if you don't know the answer?
  If you're unsure, it's better to say something like "I'll have to get back to you on that one," or "I haven't come up against that yet." Reporters can pick out the baloney a mile away.

## Talking Photos

After the boycott, Rosa Parks agreed to have her photo taken. She sat in the same seat she was removed from, her hands crossed on her lap, staring out the window. A white man sat behind her. This picture – which is simplicity itself – speaks more than a thousand words and has become a symbol of successful, non-violent, civil disobedience. Google-search "Rosa Parks' photo" and see for yourself. Do you think Rosa planned her appearance?

- Think about how you look before you're interviewed in person or if you're asked to provide a photo. Slouching on the couch in your pajamas vs. showered, dressed, and groomed?
- Dress your best by choosing colors and clothes that both flatter you and are suitable for the occasion.
- Consider the background – it conveys information too. If providing a photo of yourself, make the most of it. If you're passionate about bike lanes, be on a bike; if you love the forest, climb a tree – you get the picture.
- Reflect the right attitude. Talk to a mirror and see what others might see. How do you want to be perceived? Then write your own headline: "HOT-HEADED TREE-HUGGER SOUNDS OFF," or "THOUGHTFUL ACTIVIST HAS QUIET RESOLVE," or "IS THIS GUY FOR REAL? ACTUALLY, YES!"

# American Civil Rights

Civil rights have their roots in ancient times, when philosophers and religious leaders wrote of liberty and humanitarian values even when governed by tyrants. Today, these rights are political, legal, and social in nature. They exist so that individuals of any race, religion, sex, or political leaning can count on equality and uniformity of citizenship.

The slaves imported to the Thirteen Colonies in the early 1700s were considered property and had no rights. When slavery was abolished, civil rights did not magically appear. Here are the highs and lows in the quest for civil rights in the United States:

**A.D. 1619, United States:** American slavery begins when a Dutch ship exchanges ten African slaves for food in Jamestown, Virginia.

**A.D. 1776, United States:** The Declaration of Independence proclaims ". . . all men are created equal . . . with certain unalienable rights."

**A.D. 1807, United States:** President Thomas Jefferson, slaveholder and drafter of the declaration, signs into law a bill banning the importation of African slaves – but thousands more slaves are smuggled into the country over the next fifty years.

**A.D. 1855, United States:** A Missouri court rules that a female slave is "property," removing her right to refuse sex with her master.

**A.D. 1857, United States:** Responding to the "Dred Scott" case, Chief Justice Taney rules that all blacks living in the

United States are not, and can never become, American citizens.

**A.D. 1865, United States:** President Abraham Lincoln signs the Thirteenth Amendment to the United States Constitution, abolishing slavery. In the same year, Tennessee veterans of the Civil War found the Ku Klux Klan, vowing to uphold the rights and privileges of white Americans.

**A.D. 1870, United States:** The Fifteenth Amendment to the United States Constitution makes it illegal to prevent any citizen from voting based on "race, color or previous condition of servitude." Still, black males and all women are denied the vote for at least fifty more years because of poll taxes, literacy tests, intimidation, and discrimination.

**A.D. 1892, United States:** Homer Plessy, who is seven-eighths white, tests the Separate Car Act when he buys a first-class train ticket. He's arrested when he reveals his mixed-race heritage. When his case goes to the United States Supreme Court, he loses 7-1, and the one dissenting judge writes "Our Constitution is color-blind, and neither knows nor tolerates classes among citizens."

**A.D. 1895, United States:** Booker T. Washington, a former slave turned educator, gives his Atlanta Compromise Address, where he argues that education and employment opportunities are more valuable to his fellow blacks than social equality.

**A.D. 1925, United States:** The KKK goes national with its racist views as forty thousand Klansmen, wearing ceremonial robes, march through Washington, D.C.

**A.D. 1954, United States:** The Supreme Court rules, in the famous case of "Brown vs. Board of Education of Topeka, Kansas," that segregation in schools is unconstitutional. At the same time, the court throws out the Plessy vs. Ferguson ruling that kept the separate but equal custom in place.

**A.D. 1960, United States:** When four black students are refused service at a Greensboro, North Carolina, "whites-only" lunch counter, they begin a sit-in that gets national attention. Student sit-ins in the south and north continue until the Civil Rights Act passes in 1964, making it illegal to withhold service from anyone based on their race.

**A.D. 1968, United States:** Five years after he delivers his "I have a dream" speech, Martin Luther King Jr. is gunned down on the balcony of his motel by a white sniper, James Earl Ray.

**A.D. 1992, United States:** Twenty-five years after the Newark and Detroit race riots are sparked by police brutality, riots break out in Los Angeles. Two white police officers are acquitted in the vicious beating of African-American Rodney King. The beating is witnessed, recorded on videotape, and played on international television news.

**A.D. 2005, United States:** Rosa Parks dies at the age of ninety-two. Several days later, Montgomery and Detroit honor her by decorating the front-row seats of buses with solemn black ribbons.

**A.D. 2009, United States:** The NAACP turns one hundred. The express purpose of the organization remains "to ensure the political, educational, social, and economic equality of rights of all persons and to eliminate racial hatred and racial discrimination."

# BABY STEPS,
# GIANT LEAPS

Poppa died of lung cancer in August 1962, weighing ninety-six pounds. Janie's grandmother was furious when he smoked his pipe in hospital because she connected his illness with tobacco. But Poppa argued that the doctor smoked too. Her mom told Janie that during World War I, Poppa got cigarettes with his rations. When he was wounded, he smoked in the rehabilitation center. After he died, Janie pictured their last visit, when he'd demonstrated a new dance called the twist. His pipe was clenched in his teeth, his war-wounded leg swinging wildly. Janie knew she'd miss his dancing and his hugs that smelled of pipe tobacco.

*Or would she?* Over the next school year, Janie had "current events" homework, where she had to read the newspaper, follow an issue, and then discuss it in school. Headlines blazed: "RESEARCHER CANNOT ISOLATE CANCER AGENT BUT INSTITUTE CERTAIN OF LINK"; "CIGARETTE STARTS FIRE"; "LUNG CANCER REACHING EPIDEMIC"; "COFFIN NAILS (PUFF)"; "SEEK LABEL OF CAUTION ON CIGARETTES"; "TOBACCO INDUSTRY IS COOL TO

Warning Label Tactics"; "Cigarettes Killing More than Cars, Viruses, Cancer Expert Says."

At the grocery store, Janie hit the wall on smoking when she saw her mom buying her own dad his weekly ration of cigarettes. Armed with clippings, Janie confronted him and offered him a deal – if he quit smoking, Janie swore she'd never start. A small step in the grand scheme of things, but a step nonetheless. They composed and signed a formal document, tying it with red ribbon. Now, Dad is eighty-eight, and Janie – Jane Drake – is writing this book in a smoke-free home.

**STORY**

# Smoking vs. Nonsmoking: A Seesaw Battle of Rights

Halfway through the twentieth century, smoking was considered cool; cancer research was inconclusive; tobacco companies were bulletproof; and alarm bells silent. Over the next sixty years, all that would change. Decade-by-decade, key players and new information shaped and shifted public sentiment. Change came slowly, one small step at a time – or, one step forward, two steps back. In 2010, the rights of the nonsmoker have triumphed over those of the smoker, even though it is still legal to smoke.

During the 1950s in the United States, over fifty percent of men and about thirty-three percent of women smoked. Tobacco-industry profits soared as Camels, Lucky Strikes, Chesterfields, Commanders, and Old Gold cigarettes sold by the billions. Tobacco advertising heralded a new safer product – low-tar cigarettes with filters. Despite the filter tip, first-time smokers felt dizzy, coughed, and even vomited. As early as 1950, medical researchers in both the United States and Europe connected cigarette smoking and lung cancer. British researchers Richard Doll and Austin Bradford Hill, pioneers in the field, concluded that smokers of twenty-five cigarettes a day are fifty times more likely to get lung cancer than nonsmokers. But their own conservative Ministry of Health appeared to side with the tobacco companies – it declared the researchers may have linked smoking with lung cancer, but had failed to prove that cigarette smoking was the most significant cause.

The 1960s saw a small decline in overall smoking, but a rise in female smokers. Hollywood movies glamorized smoking in films such as *Breakfast at Tiffany's*, in which the ever-elegant Audrey Hepburn puffed from a long, sparkling cigarette holder. Still, forty-two percent of Americans smoked in 1965. Were they influenced by a handsome cowboy, riding horseback through Marlboro Country? On January 11, 1964, Surgeon General Luther Terry exposed the mounting evidence of the harmful effects of tobacco on human health. Facts were becoming clear: smoking mothers produced babies with lower birth weight; smokers' health problems went beyond the lungs and included coronary/heart complications; chronic bronchitis and emphysema were causally related to cigarette smoking. Not everyone was convinced – Dorothy Schiff, publisher of the *New York Post*, would not print stories connecting smoking with cancer. She smoked a pack of Kools every day. But Florida passed the first smoke-free laws in the United States in 1965. Big tobacco companies finally admitted their products contained the addictive chemical nicotine, but argued that the sale of cigarettes was perfectly legal.

By 1970, Congress had passed the Public Health Cigarette Smoking Act, and the U.S. smoking rate dropped to about thirty-seven percent. Cigarette labels read "WARNING: THE SURGEON GENERAL HAS DETERMINED THAT CIGARETTE SMOKING IS DANGEROUS TO YOUR HEALTH." With more adults trying to quit, Imperial Tobacco turned its sights on the youth market. One executive quipped, "The base of our business is the high-school student." One brand was specifically targeted at women: Virginia Slims advertisements linked their product to women's rights. Powerful ads sang out "You've come a long way, baby, to get where you've got to today." And with more women smoking, the rate of lung-cancer deaths in females started rising. In 1971, cigarette ads were banned from radio and TV broadcasting. But the jingles rang on – plastered across billboards and in magazines and newspapers. Partial bans were finally imposed on smoking in aircraft by 1973, and customers were given the choice, "Will that be smoking or nonsmoking?" But smoke still spread through the entire cabin, exposing passengers and flight attendants to secondhand smoke. Rosalee Berlin, a registered nurse sensitive to secondhand smoke, founded the Nonsmokers' Rights Association (NSRA) in Toronto in 1974. She crusaded for clean air in the workplace and recruited Garfield Mahood, a local environmentalist, as the executive director of NSRA. He tirelessly led the attack against Big Tobacco. Across the border in the United States, the American Cancer Society went national with its first Great American Smokeout in 1977 – a support program designed to help smokers kick the habit.

During the 1980s, while thirty-three percent of American adults smoked, lung cancer became the number one cause of death in women. And a new health issue affecting male smokers came to light as early as 1986. Urologists connected smoking and erectile dysfunction, due to decreased blood flow to the penis. In 1987, a proposed smoking ban on flights of less than two hours irritated the American tobacco industry. They argued that air travel would be unsafe as passengers would smoke in ill-equipped lavatories. In Canada, the Tobacco Products Control Act of 1988 outlawed all tobacco advertising and made health-warning labels on packaging mandatory. Meanwhile, Joe Camel – the advertising mascot camel with sunglasses and a saxophone – helped celebrate the Camel brand's seventy-fifth anniversary in 1988. Within a few years, more kids recognized him than Fred Flintstone or Mickey Mouse, but the R.J. Reynolds Tobacco Company insisted the ad did not target kids.

By 1990, about twenty-five percent of people smoked in America. But the decade turned into a tug-of-war between big business and new science. In a 1992 *Economist* article, Warren Buffet, one of the world's richest investors, commented on the tobacco industry: "I'll tell you why I like the cigarette business. It costs a penny to make. Sell it for a dollar. It's addictive. And there's fantastic brand loyalty." Groundbreaking studies in the 1990s zeroed in on children and found that ninety percent of those living with smokers were not protected from secondhand smoke. These same children missed more school with respiratory illnesses and scored lower grades than kids from nonsmoking families. In 1993, tobacco companies calculated that where smoking bans existed, the average smoker cut back by three to five cigarettes a day, butting into their profits. New medical research reported that in 1996, 2,500 Canadians died from strokes caused by smoking. Concerns for the health of its citizens prompted the Canadian government to hike taxes on cigarettes, making smoking less affordable. The result was an increase in black-market sales, and cigarette smuggling became big, dangerous business.

By 2005, seventeen percent of Americans smoked. Three years earlier, Canadian research found nicotine in the lungs of children who'd died from SIDS (Sudden Infant Death Syndrome). To protect youngsters, the Province of Newfoundland and Labrador made it illegal to smoke around children. Some businesses just banned children from their premises instead. The U.S. federal courts labeled tobacco companies racketeers for misleading the public by prominently placing words such as "light," "mild," or "low tar" on their products. In 2006, the courts ruled that all cigarettes were risky. And the surgeon general declared there was no safe level of secondhand smoke, with or without ventilation.

By 2007, there were an estimated 1.2 billion smokers in the world, smoking between 15 and 20 billion cigarettes a day. That's a lot of packaging, tobacco, paper, matches, and butts. When cigarettes are smoked, the filters in butts absorb nasty chemicals from the smoke and are now considered a form of toxic waste. Ground into the pavement, flicked into gardens, down the toilet, or into an ashtray, there is no clean way to dispose of a cigarette butt.

In 2008, the Province of Ontario introduced legislation banning smoking in cars for those driving with children. The fines it imposed were about $250.00. An outraged smoker posted a blog, wondering if banning smoking in homes was next, or if governments would take away children from parents who smoked!

Looking back, the NSRA and other antismoking groups have been responsible for a series of small changes that resulted in huge change. Smokers used to light up almost everywhere. Now, smokers shiver outside buildings, and passengers fly in smoke-free comfort. And, governments are now suing the once all-powerful tobacco companies across North America for the enormous health and social costs their products have caused. As more people butt out for the last time, we can definitely say, "We've come a long way, baby."

# *Gandhi: Non-Violent Change – One Step at a Time*

Mohandas (Mahatma) Gandhi, political and spiritual leader of India from 1915 until 1948, fought for freedom and against tyranny with non-violence. He took on the biggest power of his time, the British Empire, and he did it taking baby steps in order to make the giant leap to independence. His weapon of choice was mass civil disobedience, or passive resistance he called *satyagraha*. Even though he and his followers were utterly fed up with British rule in India, he urged non-violence as a means to freedom. He believed any change worth making should transform the heart, soul, as well as the behavior of the oppressor.

Gandhi defined *satyagraha* as the force that's born of truth and love. Certainly, it's not for cowards. He asked his followers to resist tyranny without defending themselves. He said that one couldn't achieve peace through violence nor justice through injustice. Only by expressing truth purely and without violence would oppression convert to peace and love.

A famous example of *satyagraha* was Gandhi's salt-tax protest in 1930, just after his party's pledge of independence from British rule – even though Britain still ruled. The British government held a monopoly on all production and sale of salt in India and then slapped a salt tax on top. It was ruled a crime, even for people who lived by the sea, to boil down saltwater to make salt. Salt is a critical nutrient – our muscles cannot contract without it, including our largest muscle, the heart. Human bodies do not make salt but process it out of food. And in a hot, humid country like India, people need more salt, particularly if they work outside in the sun. The salt tax hurt the poor agricultural laborers in India the most.

Gandhi wrote the British viceroy of India and said he planned to challenge and disobey the salt-tax law, unless it was changed. When no positive response came, Gandhi and eighty of his closest followers marched, for over three weeks, from their ashram to the sea. The march was well planned: forward scouts arranged for resting places, simple meals, and locations for Gandhi to address crowds. Tens of thousands of people lined the route and greeted Gandhi in the dozens of villages along the way. The international press reported daily on the progress of the march. When Gandhi reached the sea, he illegally boiled a lump of salty mud in a pail of seawater to make salt. Then he implored everyone in India to do the same.

Millions of people made salt or bought illegally made salt. The protest spread to other British-made goods. Gandhi planned a second march to a saltworks, wrote to the viceroy to advise him, but this time was arrested and imprisoned without trial for nearly a year. His wife and followers carried on with the second salt *satyagraha* and were arrested. But more of Gandhi's followers continued marching, until they were attacked and stopped by soldiers.

A United Press International correspondent reported

> "Not one of the marchers even raised an arm to fend off the blows. They went down like tenpins. From where I stood, I heard the sickening whacks of the clubs on unprotected skulls. The waiting crowd of watchers groaned and sucked in their breaths in sympathetic pain at every blow. Those struck down fell sprawling, unconscious or writhing in pain, with fractured skulls or broken shoulders. In two or three minutes, the ground was quilted with bodies. Great patches of blood widened on their white clothes. The survivors, without breaking ranks, silently and doggedly marched on until struck down."

Gandhi wasn't the first to push for independence. From 1751 onwards, uprisings, protests, and revolts all failed, ending in massacres and renewed oppression. Gandhi did not expect instant results, but patiently moved his agenda forward with persistent baby steps. *Satyagraha* gave the independence movement a huge national following and international attention – but no immediate changes to the salt tax. British rule in India did face questioning, especially in England. India finally achieved independence on August 15, 1947, and Gandhi's *satyagrahas* are credited with advancing the cause.

How did this good and powerful man of non-violence die? By the oppressor's club? No – as he walked to a prayer meeting on January 30, 1948, he was shot three times in the chest by one of his own countrymen – a man who believed Gandhi weakened India by paying Pakistan too much in the independence agreements. It was one of history's greatest ironies that a lifelong promoter of non-violence was "struck down by an assassin's bullet."

Later, civil-rights activists and organizations, including Martin Luther King Jr. and Amnesty International, studied and implemented Gandhi's ideas. But *satyagraha*, in its purest form, has not been used since with as large a group of people. Was it a form of protest that best fit the one place and one time?

**SKILLS**

# The Elements of a Good Poster/Posting

Your uncle smokes at the dining table. While your baby cousin is eating mashed peas, a cloud of smoke swirls around his little head.

This really ticks you off. How would you design a poster to raise awareness of the dangers of smoking in a confined space while kids are present? Start with the image of your cousin in his high chair, Uncle puffing away and reading the paper. . . .

You could

- Let the image do most of the talking, adding punchy statistics about secondhand smoke.
- Get at two sides of the issue – the child's right to safety and the father's obligation to provide a safe environment for his child – with an effective caption, such as READ HIM HIS RIGHTS.
- Use your own creative ideas.

### Easy Reading

Draft your poster or posting on a computer. Step back from the screen and ask yourself, "Is this easy to read?"

- Use a big, clean, simple font. Curly q's and fancy scripts will distract the reader and detract from your message.
- Highlight or bold your most important points.
- Check the web for great tips on graphic design. Did you know that people don't remember white text on a dark background or text in ALL CAPITAL LETTERS?

### Eye-catching

Be different and fresh in the design of your poster. Draw from your own daring and creative side, without copying other people's ideas. Design's first task is to grab the eye and reach the brain.

- Say as much as you can with the illustration or graphics, and then play with blocks of very limited text until they are arranged logically and attractively. Your message should flow across and around the page.

- Leave white/empty spaces so that your reader's eyes will concentrate on the important information.
- Use color and contrast to influence the reader and enhance your message. Green will evoke nature and environmental concern; red is an eye-stopper; black and white, a harsh reality.
- Don't overuse the exclamation mark. A few well-chosen words should do the work!!!

## Right to the Point

Ads are everywhere. Some are annoying, some are confusing, and others get to you instantly. Take a leaf out of a slick advertising campaign and go for the big punch.

Be precise. Someone looking at your poster/posting will pause for only a few seconds. If they're interested, they'll read it. Otherwise, it's click, click, bye.

Do several drafts and ask for a peer review. It's easy to become satisfied with your own work, while perhaps you've overlooked something obvious or necessary. You may make assumptions in the viewer's understanding, confusing instead of informing him.

## Sense Appeal

Close your eyes and picture a loon swimming on a pristine lake. Does it take you to the wild? A basket of newborn puppies? *Ahh!* How about a polar bear falling through the ice? Does it warn of global warming? Posters are seen with the eyes, but can appeal to all the senses and emotions too. Choose images and words that prompt the response you are after.

### The Post with the Most

Time and place are key elements in a story. The same is true for where and when you launch your poster/posting. Maximize your impact by knowing what's happening in your community. Don't get lost in the hubbub of a holiday, other event, or issue. Avoid making a negative impact by defacing property or illegally posting. Place your poster where it's permitted to be and easy to read. Try to make it front and center and attention-grabbing. To get the attention of your

- Principal – tape the poster to his/her door before the bell. Catch this busy person before the phone starts ringing and the day gets crazy.
- Teachers – place your poster on the staff-lounge door before lunch. Get your teachers when they're converging on one place, so they'll talk about your issue.
- Parents – be direct, but polite. You want them to take your cause or concerns seriously.
- Siblings – interrupt a familiar routine, if you are trying to change patterns.
- Friends – plaster your Facebook wall before the weekend begins. Choose a time when you'll catch the most friends on the net, then reel them in.

**TIMELINE**  *MILESTONES AND SETBACKS*

# Tobacco and Nonsmokers' Rights

As far back as 6000 B.C., early peoples in the Americas cultivated the tobacco plant. They smoked for pleasure, ceremony, and medicinal purposes – even using tobacco in enemas. In the fifteenth century, Columbus' diary records that he was given a gift of "certain dried leaves" in San Salvador, but he threw them away. When his ship returned to Spain, Rodrigo de Jeres, a crew member who brought tobacco home, was imprisoned for smoking. The Inquisition accused him of being possessed by the devil.

Smoking tobacco gradually caught on worldwide, taking centuries for its harmful effects to be recognized. In hindsight, we should have known that where there's smoke, there's fire:

**A.D. 1571, England:** Doctor Nicolas Monardes' treatise on medicinal tobacco use proclaims smoking cures more than sixty-five diseases.

**c. A.D. 1580, England:** Sir Walter Raleigh introduces and popularizes tobacco use in Elizabeth I's court. In 1618, he's granted one last smoke of Virginia pipe tobacco before being beheaded.

**c. A.D. 1600, India, China, Japan, Turkey, Korea, Russia, Mongolia:** Smoking is banned. Punishments include slitting smokers' lips, whippings, banishment, and execution.

**A.D. 1604, England:** King James I makes his feelings clear when he writes "Smoking is a custom loathsome to the eye, hateful to the nose, harmful to the brain, dangerous to the lungs, and in the black, stinking fume thereof nearest resembling the horrible Stygian smoke of the pit that is bottomless."

**A.D. 1619, United States:** Tobacco is accepted as a currency in Virginia. Jamestown settlers pay for their wives' boat passage from England with 120 pounds of tobacco.

**c. A.D. 1700, United States:** The labor of slaves is used in the cultivation of tobacco.

**A.D. 1795, Germany:** Dr. Samuel Thomas von Söemmering connects lip cancer with pipe-smoking.

**A.D. 1828, Germany:** Chemistry students in Heidelberg break down the elements in tobacco smoke and declare nicotine a "dangerous poison."

**c. A.D. 1890, Indonesia:** The inventors of clove-infused or "kretek" cigarettes claim them to be soothing for asthmatics.

**c. A.D. 1890, United States:** Author Mark Twain comments on his addiction: "To quit smoking is one of the easiest things in the world. I must have done it over a dozen times."

**A.D. 1924, United States:** A *Reader's Digest* article entitled "Does Tobacco Injure the Human Body?" challenges people to think before they smoke.

**A.D. 1995, United States:** David McLean, the "Marlboro Man," dies of lung cancer forty-one years after first appearing in a Philip Morris cigarette advertisement.

**A.D. 2000, Japan:** Emperor Akihito celebrates his birthday without giving free cigarettes to his staff, ending a thirty-eight-year tradition.

**A.D. 2004, Ireland:** A smoking ban in pubs, restaurants, and workplaces results in a 7.5% drop in cigarette consumption in the first six months.

**A.D. 2004, Norway:** Airport posters announce a ban on smoking: "Welcome to Norway. The only thing we smoke here is salmon."

**A.D. 2009, United States:** Still trying to quit, President Obama says he'll honor the smoking ban while living in the White House.

# BUTTING
# HEADS

**S**lip a driver's license into your wallet for the first time – and feel the freedom. You've come of age, at last!

On November 16, 2008, the government of Ontario introduced legislation to diminish and delay that achievement. Drivers under the age of twenty-one, who had earned an intermediate-stage license permitting them to drive without in-car supervision, faced three new restrictions. They would lose their license if caught driving under any of these conditions:

- above the speed limit
- with *any* alcohol in their system, even if of legal drinking age
- with more than one passenger under the age of nineteen (not including family) in the car during their first year.

The government cited statistics showing that young drivers cause more fatal accidents than any other age group and that the more teens there are in a car, the greater the chance of a crash.

Parents who had lost children in horrific young-driver accidents stood beside the premier when he announced the proposed legislation.

Kids could swallow the first two restrictions, but the third seemed outrageous. Speeding was against the law anyway, and everyone knew the toxic relationship between drinking and driving. Surely there was another way to train young drivers to deal with responsibilities and distractions than by forbidding them to have more than one teenage passenger. How were young people going to find designated drivers on nights out? How were rural teens going to get to extracurricular activities?

Both sides had the best of intentions and thought their concerns were the most important. Government and parents versus kids – who wins that battle?

On the heels of the announcement, determined teens started a protest on the Internet. They set up an online petition and a Facebook group dedicated to their objections. All protesters had an opportunity to air their opinions, voice their concerns, and be counted. The news media were fascinated and reported on the rising number of members in the Facebook group and what kids were saying. In less than three weeks, 150,000 had joined the online protests. On December 8, the government removed the unwanted restriction from their legislation. Against all odds, young people found a powerful, public way to be heard.

This confrontation was a lot more pleasant than some. Prepare yourself for conflict, and use a power struggle – butting heads – to benefit your cause.

# Greenpeace vs. the American Military

In January 1969, Richard Nixon became the president of the United States and the most powerful man in the world. His country was at war on two fronts: on the ground in Vietnam and head-to-head in a nuclear arms race with Russia, known as the Cold War. In a dramatic show of strength, the American military scheduled an underground atomic bomb test for October on the island of Amchitka, in the Aleutian Islands off Alaska.

In Vancouver, British Columbia, a group of friends – and friends of friends – started to discuss this proposed Amchitka nuclear test informally, meeting in a local pub or in homes nearby. Although most of the group were in their early twenties, several were older, and one was a World War II veteran. Some joined the discussions because they felt any weapons-testing escalated the chance of all-out war. Others were Vietnam draft resisters who wanted Americans to rethink the growing military/industrial machine. A number were pacifists of the Quaker faith, who deeply believed in bearing witness, in a non-violent way, to any assault on Mother Earth. Environmentalists joined in because Amchitka Island was a national wildlife refuge, home to one of the last significant populations of endangered sea otters. Together, these diverse groups shared fears for the safety of any test because Amchitka lies in an earthquake zone. Could the blast trigger serious radiation leaks and tidal waves? They eventually decided to protest the upcoming Amchitka nuclear test together, in a non-violent way. They believed that it had to be stopped for the good of humanity and of Earth.

Meanwhile, American casualties escalated in Vietnam, and the Cold War ramped up. The People's Republic of China supported American enemies in Vietnam while Russia was the main adversary in the Cold War. Both China and Russia ran nuclear-testing programs. The U.S. president and generals believed America had every right to protect itself by building up its weapons capabilities. Amchitka lay almost as far west as Asia. By choosing this remote island for their test, the military reduced the risk to American people while keeping the test on American soil. They were outraged that American draft resisters and Canadian "radicals" dared question their right to test a bomb in their own country. The government was convinced its weapons-testing program was for the good of the American people.

On October 1, 1969, the protest group carried signs that read DON'T MAKE A WAVE and marched at the United States/Canada border south of Vancouver with busloads of university students. On schedule, the one-megaton bomb detonated 1,220 m (about 4,000 ft.) under the island of Amchitka. At the University of Victoria, in British Columbia, the shockwave measured 6.9 on the Richter scale. In fact, it was felt by earthquake-detecting instruments around the world. At ground zero, the surface of the earth arched 5 m (16.4 ft.) high, in a dome with a radius of about 3 km (1.9 mi.). Rivers and lakes gushed 15 m (49.2 ft.) into the air like geysers; the ocean frothed; and unknown numbers of wild birds, seals, sea otters, and other sea creatures died. The surface of the island above ground zero then collapsed, leaving a crater, as rock and debris settled into the cavity blasted out below.

Almost immediately, the American military announced that in the fall of 1971, they would detonate another bomb, this time a five-megaton nuclear warhead, under the same island. The core group of Vancouver protesters formed the Don't Make a Wave Committee to stop it. But for several months, the committee couldn't come up with a good strategy.

On a February morning in 1970, Marie Bohlen and her husband,

Jim, Quaker pacifists and members of the committee, drank coffee and worried that the protest was going nowhere. Suddenly Marie thought *Why doesn't the committee just charter a boat and sail to Amchitka to confront and bear witness to the next detonation?* The phone rang; it was a news reporter wanting to know if Jim could give him a story. Jim told the reporter about Marie's idea before he had a chance to tell the other committee members, but that didn't kill the committee's enthusiasm. It held an emergency meeting to consider the idea. At the end of the meeting, one of the members flashed the peace sign and said, "Peace." Another member, Bill Darnell, said, "Make it a *green* peace." Like Marie's sudden inspirational suggestion to charter a boat, Bill's casual comment took hold, and soon people were calling the yet-to-be-chartered boat the *Green Peace.*

For the next year, the Don't Make a Wave Committee raised money, made plans, kept the news media interested, and searched for the right boat. They settled on a 20 m (65.6 ft.) halibut fishing seiner called the *Phyllis McCormack*, after the wife of the captain. John McCormack had forty years sailing experience on the West Coast. He needed money because fishing for halibut had not been good recently, and he was prepared to sail to Amchitka for $12,000.00 (plus fuel costs) in time for the blast, scheduled for October 2, 1971. Settling on a crew took time, but on September 15, the boat, rechristened the *Greenpeace* for this trip, left Vancouver with a seasoned captain and a crew of activists.

Politicians and military personnel dismissed the crew of the *Greenpeace* as a group of hippies and radicals. John Wayne, a famous American actor, called them a bunch of Communists. However, among them were four reporters who knew how to reach the public: Robert Hunter wrote a column for the *Vancouver Sun*; Ben Metcalfe worked for both the *Province* and the *Canadian Broadcasting*

*Corporation*; Bob Cummings wrote for an underground newspaper, the *Georgia Strait*; and Robert Kaziere was a photojournalist.

As the *Greenpeace* sailed north and west, armed with a radio-dispatch unit, the world took notice. The American military prepared for their test deadline and tracked the passage of the protest boat. Reporters on board the *Greenpeace* issued daily stories that were hungrily listened to and read around the world.

When the *Greenpeace* was only three days from Amchitka Island, President Nixon delayed the test, a strategy no one on board had expected. The captain and crew decided to put into an island half-way down the Aleutian chain and take on provisions. The coast guard gave them permission to anchor off the small city of Akutan. Permission to anchor, as the protesters eventually found out, was not permission to go ashore. As the *Greenpeace* prepared to leave Akutan to wait it out at Amchitka, a United States Coast Guard vessel, the *Confidence*, arrived in the harbor. The commander boarded the *Greenpeace* and charged Captain McCormack for not making a formal entry application with U.S. Customs, on behalf of his crew, within forty-eight hours of landing at Akutan. The *Greenpeace* had to return to the mainland to face charges and fines.

While the commander of the *Confidence* spoke to Captain McCormack, the *Confidence* crew handed the *Greenpeace* crew a signed note, saying they were behind the protesters one hundred percent. And it took no time for journalists on board the *Greenpeace* to read the note and names of the signatories over the radio to news media back home.

The *Greenpeace* sailed for Vancouver. The United States Supreme Court denied an injunction to stop the test, filed by concerned American pacifists, in a 4-3 decision. A Canadian petition of 177,000 signatures opposing the test was delivered to the White House, while Sweden, Peru, and Japan raised diplomatic objections to it.

But President Nixon rescheduled the blast for November 6. Two days before the test, the head of the Atomic Energy Commission, his wife, and child flew to Amchitka Island to sit out the bomb in a bunker. On the morning of November 6, bridges between Canada and the United States were blocked with protesters, church bells rang out in protest, but the bomb went off as scheduled.

This time, the blast sent a shockwave registering 7.0 on the Richter scale. At ground zero, the earth lifted 6 m (19.7 ft.); giant rockfalls and turf slides occurred over its dome; the ocean frothed; two thousand sea otters died; and a new mile-long lake formed in the crater left when the surface subsided. But there were no tidal waves.

In February 1972, the American military announced it would abandon the Amchitka test site for "political and other reasons." The Don't Make a Wave Committee – soon to become Greenpeace – had lost the battle, but had made its point against the biggest military power the world had ever known.

**STRATEGIES**

## *Burnout*

Burnout, or loss of motivation from prolonged frustration or stress, is a nasty side effect of working hard for an ideal. Burnout comes in increasing degrees of seriousness and can show up in different ways. Telltale signs include

- exhaustion – a loss of energy and enthusiasm
- self-pity – a feeling of not being listened to, even by your supporters and co-workers

- resentment – a feeling of indignance, or believing you are the only one who actually does anything
- crankiness – exhibiting anger when opposed, from making a few sarcastic wisecracks to snarling tirades
- loss of perspective – a conviction that nothing in life matters but the cause.

In any form, burnout is bad news. It can destroy what you have built, and it can destroy your personal life. Robert Hunter, one of the founders of Greenpeace, commented on the toll the protests took on his family and relationships in his book *The Greenpeace to Amchitka: An Environmental Odyssey.*

The best remedy to burnout is to avoid it altogether. Look after yourself and encourage your fellow change-makers to do the same.

- Take time off to rebuild reserves of energy. Have a life.
- Book fun time with co-workers. No work agenda allowed.
- Celebrate even small victories. They are steps forward.
- Keep a running list of accomplishments to record how far you have come. Have perspective.
- Talk about burnout with co-workers, family, and friends, so you recognize it when it strikes.

**SKILLS**

## *Sharpening Your Tongue*

The battle lines are drawn – you and your opposition know where each other stands. Are you ready for a face-to-face, head-to-head confrontation? It may occur at a public meeting, on a radio show, in a formal debate, on the Internet, or one-on-one. You can prepare, well ahead of time, a basic pitch and good rebuttals to what you think will be your opponents' comebacks.

First, have your pitch ready in concise and logical form. Include

- significant problems with the current situation, *aka* the status quo
- your proposed change
- benefits of your proposed change
- your vision of the situation after your proposed change
- names of reliable experts who endorse your assessments and/or solutions
- a restatement of your proposed change, presented in a slightly new way.

Then role-play:

- Have a friend listen to your pitch and make suggestions to improve it.
- Have a friend respond as if he or she were your opposition. Practice responding to the arguments and comments your friend fires back.
- Reverse roles. Put yourself into the opposition's shoes and keep track of your best verbal shots.
- Ask an elder – such as your parent or grandparent – to play the opposition. Consider their arguments, comments, and responses.
- Compile a list of arguments your opposition might use against you and come up with good counterarguments. Practice them out loud, speaking into a mirror.

Learn to spot manipulative tactics, so you can point them out as irrelevant:

- Name-calling: your argument is diminished, simplified, and dismissed by turning you (and your allies) into a caricature or stereotype based on
  - your age, gender, ethnicity, appearance, clothing, level of education ("long-haired anarchist," "sandals and T-shirt type," "weirdo do-gooder," "redneck," "egghead" . . .)
  - the intensity of your concern ("snitch," "fusspot," "gossip," "meddler" . . .)
  - the nature of your concern ("tree-hugger," "left-wing socialist," "granola head" . . .)
- Red herrings: your argument is attacked by irrelevant appeals, such as
  - tradition ("What would your grandmother say?")
  - patriotism ("If you really loved your country . . .")
  - emotion ("But what about all the people suffering [in another place, from another issue] . . .")
- False logic: your argument is dismissed by
  - forcing a limited choice, when several are possible ("It's either owls or jobs . . .")
  - making a false comparison or analogy, often misusing statistics ("More sixteen-year-olds will be struck by lightning this year than will die from tobacco-related illness" or "Cigarettes can kill you, yes, but you can also die from eating too much chocolate . . .")
  - taking your point to the extreme ("If one person gets special treatment, then . . .")
  - minimizing ("You are making a big deal out of nothing . . .")

Use of manipulative devices is not always obvious – watch for "gray" ones. Respond by pointing out the stereotyping, irrelevancies, and/or false logic and move on.

# *Earth Rights*

Greenpeace is the present-day expression of an Earth rights movement that reaches back into very early times. Is it possible that now, more than ever, people value peace in combination with a respect for all creatures and peoples?

**527 B.C., India:** Mahavira, the founder of Jainism, dies. His conversion to vegetarianism as a way to avoid animal slaughter and express compassion for all living beings spreads, over time, among Hindus and Buddhists.

**A.D. 1226, Italy:** Francis of Assisi dies after a life devoted to rescuing and caring for animals and birds. Reportedly, he even made peace between villagers, their dogs, and a ravenous wolf.

**A.D. 1682, United States:** William Penn and the Society of Friends (Quakers) found the colony of Pennsylvania on principles of non-violence and respect for the land: they walk among native peoples unarmed, purchase land fairly, and trade without carrying weapons.

**A.D. 1818, England:** Mary Shelley writes *Frankenstein*, a gothic novel that explores the ethical problems of science creating life.

**A.D. 1902, United States:** President Theodore Roosevelt

refuses to shoot a young bear his hunting guides tie to a tree to give him an easy shot. A New York shopkeeper names stuffed toy bears teddy bears to capitalize on the media buzz the story creates.

**A.D. 1957, Norway:** Dr. Albert Schweitzer, a Nobel Peace Prize laureate, calls for the end of all nuclear testing. He is ridiculed by military leaders for saying that a nuclear war will have no victors, only losers.

**A.D. 1963, Russia:** The United States, the Soviet Union (USSR), and the United Kingdom sign a nuclear-test-ban treaty that stops above-ground, outer-space, and underwater nuclear testing.

**A.D. 1970, United States:** The first Earth Day is celebrated on April 22.

**A.D. 1972, Outer Space:** The *Apollo 17* spacecraft crew photograph Earth from a distance of 29,000 km (18,000 mi.). The image, called the Blue Marble, becomes a stark reminder of the finite nature of planet Earth.

**A.D. 1979, Atlantic Ocean:** Greenpeace member Paul Watson rams the Portuguese pirate whaler the *Sierra* with his boat on the high seas. Watson goes on to sink or damage other pirate whalers to protest the Newfoundland seal hunt and to campaign for the end to drift-net fishing in the Pacific.

**A.D. 1982, United States:** The UN passes the World Charter for Nature, officially recognizing the right to survival and protection to organisms, natural habitats, and processes. All member countries sign the charter except the United States.

**A.D. 1994, England:** The London Convention, an international agreement among eighty-six countries to stop the dumping of waste at sea, now includes the dumping of radioactive material as waste.

**A.D. 2007, Australia:** WWF organizes a global event called Earth Hour. Families and businesses turn off lights and appliances for one specified hour in March to make the connection between energy use and climate change.

**A.D. 2007, Norway:** American Al Gore shares the Nobel Peace Prize for his efforts to increase the world's understanding of climate change and what is needed to stop global warming.

**A.D. 2009, Earth Orbit:** Guy Laliberté, founder of Cirque de Soleil, enters the International Space Station, intending to raise global awareness of water conservation and to pass around clown noses to the astronauts and cosmonauts on board.

# WHEN THE GOING GETS TOUGH, THE TOUGH GET GOING

"**A**nd now, what you've all been waiting for – the results of the student presidential election. It looked like it would be too close to call, but we do have a victor. Your next president is . . ." The principal brandished a sheet of paper as if announcing an Oscar winner. Everyone leaned forward. Would it be Ab or Martin? "Please put your hands together for your democratically elected Ab Jangda."

Ab was stunned. His friends and supporters dragged him to his feet and shoved him towards the stage, clapping and yelling. This was surreal.

Ab's mind buzzed with memories of the nasty campaign. There was the day he'd arrived at school and nearly every locker had his baby photo on it with a caption that read "BABY JANGDA DROOLS, BUT CAN HE RULE?" They'd made fun of his lack of facial hair – not nearly as manly as Martin's goatee. He'd been labeled computer nerd and chess geek, while Martin's face shone down from every team photo that lined the halls. *Martin's always the MVP, captain, and record breaker. And he's part of the in crowd. So why'd they elect me?* Ab wondered. And now the principal's voice was announcing that Martin would be his vice president. They'd have to work together. *This isn't going to be a walk on the red carpet*, thought Ab as he shook hands with the principal and his new VP. Somehow he'd suck it up, forget the past, and work with this guy. Meanwhile Martin looked Ab straight in the eye and nodded, knowing he could whup Ab's butt on every other playing field. It was game on. . . .

Will Ab make a difference in his high school? Success may depend on how he's prepared to deal with those people who try to discredit him or derail his plans. Don't sweat the small stuff, Ab. Avoid unnecessary power struggles while recognizing some conflict is necessary to effect change. Ab will have to learn patience – change is not a linear process. He'll hit some bumps in the road – can he hang in there and have the guts to hold on through rough times? Ab will do well to listen to and respect others' opinions. And he'll need to toughen up and not take things personally. It's about issues, not people.

**STORY**

## *Eglantyne and Dorothy Jebb: Founders of Save the Children*

Here's the scene: It's World War I in England, and the government tightly controls all media. The content of posters, leaflets, radio shows, and films must be approved and shown to boost morale, encourage recruitment into the war effort, or channel negative feelings towards "the enemy." As war drags on and casualties rise, young men are conscripted – forced – to enlist. With troops to feed and the enemy blockading imports, British citizens are asked to cut back on food and beer. As staples become scarcer, compulsory rationing is imposed. Meanwhile, England and her allies blockade the kaiser's Germany and his empire, making life a struggle for everyone there, including children. Basic food and medicine are cut off.

Enter Eglantyne and Dorothy Jebb, with plans to change attitudes towards enemy children and send relief into a war zone. *Feed the enemy? Were they joking?* The sisters were dead serious, and the results of their efforts are still impacting children trapped in turmoil to this day.

The Jebb women were predisposed to getting involved and wanting to make a difference. Dorothy and Eglantyne had been raised with strong female role models in a time when women did not have the vote. Their mother was a social worker, their aunt a suffragette and freethinker. Biographers suggest Eglantyne was a dreamer, but she obviously chose action when Dorothy brought restricted photos into England that showed the misery of so-called "enemy" children. Eglantyne was quoted as saying, "All wars are waged against children." With this in mind, she pushed the British public out of their comfort zone by distributing images of starving Austrian children. She was arrested, but at her court hearing, she managed to squeeze a donation out of the prosecutor's pocket before paying a fine of five pounds!

Eglantyne joined the Fight the Famine Council and pressured the British government to lift the blockade. Dorothy suggested they concentrate their efforts on the young and vulnerable, so they founded Save the Children in May 1919. From today's perspective, this seems like a no-brainer. But their work was seen as near-treason, and some tried to discredit their cause.

At times, their confidence wobbled, but Eglantyne and Dorothy kept their focus by concentrating on their message.

One night, the Jebb sisters spoke to a group gathered in London's Royal Albert Hall. Eglantyne spoke, knowing in advance that the group was hostile and prepared to disrupt her by throwing rotten apples. She was so passionate and convincing that the audience held the apples back and listened.

Eglantyne became a fundraising magician, whose goal of reaching beyond her own country was set: "We have to devise means of making known the facts in such a way as to touch the imagination of the world." Starting with her own donation of ten pounds, her organization collected 72 million pounds in the years following WW I – an enormous sum for the day. And it was the first to raise funds by asking donors to individually sponsor a child – a strategy that's still effective today. She believed in having expert advice and hired a manager who used another novel concept – newspaper advertising – to attract donors.

Eglantyne Jebb's philosophy was that aid should be active, not static. Looking beyond the current crisis, she proposed that relief should have follow-up – including agricultural training and donations of tools and seeds. Her commitment had a goal beyond gesture: to assist individuals or groups to move forward on their own. "Help should not be a gift," she said, "but rather help aimed at self-help between equals, where everyone contributes according to their ability from a feeling of human fellowship across racial, ethnic, and national borders."

Believing the world to be responsible for the protection of children everywhere, Eglantyne Jebb sketched out on paper the first "Rights of the Child," breaking these rights down into five elements.

In the language of her time, she stated that all children must be

- given the means to develop normally – physically and spiritually
- fed, nursed, helped when backward, reclaimed when delinquent, sheltered and nurtured if orphaned or abandoned
- the first recipients of help in all disasters
- educated to protect themselves from exploitation
- taught to help others.

After clearing many hurdles to establish Save the Children, Eglantyne thought their organization would be needed for only two years. But it endures to this day as a well-respected and much-needed NGO (Non-Government Organization). In 2009, the Save the Children Fund operated in 130 countries worldwide, responding to current and ongoing disasters that engulf children. From the beginning, it was a reactive organization, acting when and where necessity demanded – from victims in revolutionary Russia to hungry kids of the Great Depression in the Appalachian Valley to tsunami victims of Southeast Asia and more. Eglantyne Jebb died in 1928, but her life formed the building blocks for the ongoing work of the Save the Children Fund.

## STRATEGIES

# *The Power of Petition: Children's Rights Club, Makari, Haiti*

Save the Children and other organizations concerned with child welfare initiate, sponsor, and support Children's Rights Clubs in places such as Kenya, Ethiopia, India, and Haiti. Club activities are designed to help kids understand their rights and give them a voice to speak up with when these rights are violated or neglected.

During a July 2009 site visit to Haiti, David Morley, president and CEO of Save the Children Canada, learned firsthand that the Makari Children's Rights Club is more than doing its job. A few years ago, his colleagues were served a formal petition from the children of Makari. *Why*, they asked, *did they not have their own school when education is a fundamental right? How could they work on the family farm and study if they had to walk through rivers and along impassible roads two hours each way to the closest school?* Save the Children worked with the community to make change happen. Land was donated and parents laid a foundation for the building; Save the Children built the first three classrooms and bathrooms. Meanwhile, benches and books and a dilapidated building damaged in the last hurricane became a temporary village school for over two hundred kids. The parents hired a local man who had studied at teacher's college in Port-au-Prince and agreed to pay him and his teachers directly. And the parents are taking lessons themselves – grade one is taught in the evenings, so the adults can keep up with the kids!

Petitions date back to the days of the Egyptian pharaohs, Imperial China, Elizabethan England, up to modern times. Considered a fundamental civil right in the free world, citizens can petition their governments as individuals or as groups. A petition provides an avenue for addressing complaints or concerns that can be personal or for society at large. They are a classic, non-violent way of being heard and asking for change.

Using a petition, the Children's Rights Club of Makari has become a powerful engine for social change. With the second half of the construction on the school started in fall 2009, Eglantyne Jebb might see this happening exactly as it should – people helping others to help themselves. And David Morley is carrying forward her vision when he quips, "Maybe that's a big part of children's rights – helping them as they lead, as they carve their own path and find a way to be active participants in our rapidly changing world. By focusing on rights and building on strengths instead of seeing only the needs, which are obvious, we can find a way to support people in Makari as they strive to meet the challenges of the world today."

## SKILLS

# *Finding the Fundraiser in You*

One of the hardest things about changing the world is raising money to support your cause. Thinking, planning, and time are required to coax money away from donors. Even when you run a fundraiser that's frivolous or fun, there is always a serious subtext. And you need to speak to the serious side of donors by providing inspiring information about your cause, keeping in mind that raising funds goes hand in hand with raising awareness. When you make a direct connection between the event and the cause, your sponsors will be informed and engaged. Popular examples of such events include JUMP ROPE FOR HEART (exercise is good for the heart); the TERRY FOX RUN (Terry himself ran about halfway across Canada to raise money for cancer research); and PADDLE THE DON (money raised helps clean up Toronto's Don River).

Whether you want to contribute to an existing charity or establish one of your own, think big but start small. A coin drive may sound insignificant, but professional fundraisers will tell you that every donation counts. Recently, a class from Knoxdale Public

School in Ottawa held a coin drive in support of victims of Cyclone Nargis in Myanmar. One student read about the plight of the children there and brought his concerns to class. Everyone participated, and soon they had twenty-two thousand coins to sort and roll. They chose the charity Save the Children to put their $1,100.00 to work fast.

## Raising Funds for Established Charities

After you've picked a cause, make phone or E-mail contact with their fundraising person.

- Ask how your money will be spent and what percentage is spent on administration.
- Ask if they have tried-and-true fundraising methods.
- Share any new ideas with them and offer to work together. Most charities love young people to engage with them. Make meaningful connections and learn from each other.
- Look for something to celebrate within your cause, such as an anniversary: In 2011, the World Wildlife Fund turns fifty, and pandas still need your help. Donors like specific goals and reasons for giving money.

## What's in It for Me?

Beware of the giveaway gimmick. If you donate time, money, and thought to a worthwhile cause, suggest that you don't need a freebie to make you feel good. A simple thank-you has no footprint and creates good feeling, not trash.

## School Fundraising

You've probably been involved in some form of fundraising – selling cookies, wrapping paper, chocolate bars, etc. If you want to introduce a new initiative at your school, there's definitely a process.

- Get like-minded friends involved and form a committee.
- Meet with the school administration and establish permission and rapport.
- Request time/permission to make an announcement over the school's PA system.
- Add a blurb to an online newsletter to trumpet your fundraising project.
- Do a thirty-second dramatic presentation during a school assembly, making everyone aware of your cause.
- Set a time limit for your campaign.
- Count your pennies!

Follow up with a bulletin letting all contributors know how much was raised and how it's going to help.

### United Way Week at Northern Secondary School

Participating in an annual event is one way to make a contribution. That's what kids at Northern Secondary School (NSS) in Toronto do. And while changing the world can be a daunting task, they've managed to turn fundraising for a great cause into an energized schoolwide endeavor.

NSS has been raising money for the United Way for over ten years. The school starts gearing up in September, when each class brainstorms a fundraising gimmick. The idea is to "power fundraise," using snippets of non-academic time – before and after school, at lunchtime, and in the evening. While attendance is being taken, you can pay two dollars and send a personal serenade-o-gram to a friend in another class. At lunch, the Girls Athletic

Association serves up grilled-cheese sandwiches for a few dollars. After school, for a nominal fee, a personal attendant in a gorilla suit can carry your backpack to the bus stop.

The United Way Week Committee has a modest budget for funding classes that buy supplies – spend a little, make a lot. Local businesses give generously, and students dig deep into their collective network of connections and borrow key equipment to save costs. For instance, last year a loaned cotton-candy machine was set up in the front hall. There was a fall-fair atmosphere as students lined up for the sweet-tasting fluff. Another class set up a barbecue on the front lawn, while another sold smoothies and milkshakes. Food is always popular!

One night, the auditorium was packed for an exclusive viewing of *Jurassic Park* on the big screen. And jumbo bags of popcorn were on sale. But the kids who raised the most money were in the computer science homeroom. They'd transformed the lab into a games arcade, charging admission for each half hour of playing time.

Every year features a fantastic fashion show, with student designers, fashion models, stage crew, and emcees. The show takes weeks to organize and runs for two sold-out performances. To participate, the teachers put on Faculty Follies – skits written and performed by the staff. Another source of hilarity during the week comes at unexpected moments, when the drama club's improv team does spontaneous stand-up comedy in the halls. Then they pass the hat.

A popular recent addition is a relay event where sponsored students walk or run the track for twenty-four hours. If that doesn't wear them out, they can also join in the annual climb of the CN Tower – Canada's tallest freestanding structure – getting donations for each step of the way.

Each year, the teachers initiate United Way Week, reminding the students of past glories and the school's reputation for goals reached. It is a point of great school pride that NSS was nominated for the United Way Spirit Award in 2004 and 2008, winning it for three consecutive years, from 2005–2007. Now the students want to get back on track with record-breaking donations to the United Way Campaign.

United Way is an international nonprofit organization that works one dollar and one volunteer at a time. It focuses on communities where poverty and dislocation make getting ahead difficult, especially for youth. Donations go towards funding a variety of projects, such as helping kids who live in under-serviced communities to plant and tend organic gardens. Harvested food is either taken home or shared in a community kitchen. Projects like this help young people fit in by participating and being part of a group. And they learn a thing or two about good nutrition.

If you'd like to start a United Way Week at your school, check out "youthunited" on the United Way website. It provides an A–Z of activity ideas – some regularly used by NSS students. There is something to appeal to everyone, including paying a dollar for such things as

- a tune spun by a DJ
- your very own fortune, told by tarot cards, a crystal ball, or your horoscope
- guessing the celebrity in the look-alike contest
- participating in ridiculous Olympics, such as air guitaring, yodeling, or three-legged races
- joining a pumpkin-carving contest with donated pumpkins
- voting for the funniest school video.

With some imaginative planning, you and your fellow students will have fun while raising money.

# Women and Children's Rights

If you look carefully at the history of human rights, you'll notice that these rights usually refer to the "man" part of human. England's Magna Carta established rights for "free men" that were above the rule of the king. Specific rights for women and children have been put into law very recently – but not in all countries.

**A.D. 1776, United States:** Founding Father John Adams, signatory of the Declaration of Independence, receives a note from his wife, Abigail: "Remember the Ladies, and be more generous and favorable to them than your ancestors."

**A.D. 1791, France:** Feminist pioneer Olympe de Gouges pens the Declaration of the Rights of Woman and the Female Citizen, urging French women to challenge male authority. She is beheaded by guillotine in 1793 for her outspoken views during the French Revolution.

**A.D. 1797, England:** Mary Wollstonecraft dies from complications after giving birth to her second child. She's famous for saying, "I do not wish [women] to have power over men, but over themselves."

**A.D. 1837–39, England:** Charles Dickens exposes the underbelly of his society – poverty and criminal abuse of children – in his serial novel *Oliver Twist.*

**A.D. 1839, United States:** Mississippi becomes the first state to make it legal for a white married woman to own property – but she still needs her husband's permission. In 1900, New York leads the way with a law giving women control over their wages and property, but today, there are still parts of the world where women can't work or own anything.

**A.D. 1853, United States:** Charles Loring Brace founds the Children's Aid Society, aiming to place homeless children in a family setting. Between 1854 and 1929, his Orphan Train Movement transports an estimated two hundred thousand abused, abandoned, or orphaned children across the country, finding them adoptive families along the way.

**A.D. 1854, United States:** Organized charitable nurseries (day cares) open, allowing women to work outside the home. By 2008, women make up 46.5 percent of the workforce.

**A.D. 1869, United States:** The Territory of Wyoming passes the first female suffrage law.

**A.D. 1916, United States:** Margaret Sanger opens the first American birth-control clinic, in Brooklyn, New York, on October 16th. Nine days later, the police close it down, and Sanger serves thirty days in jail.

**A.D. 1918, United States:** It's illegal for married women to use contraceptives in America. By the 1950s, Canadian women can buy contraceptives, but it's illegal for their doctors to advise them to do so.

**A.D. 1979, United States:** UNESCO announces the first International Year of the Child, focusing world attention on the needs of children.

**A.D. 1979, United States:** An international women's bill of rights, the UN Convention on the Elimination of All Forms of Discrimination Against Women, is signed into law. Three Islamic member states never sign, nor do several Pacific island states and the Vatican City.

**A.D. 1990, Iraq:** Saddam Hussein uses women and children as human shields to deter military strikes from Israel.

Thirteen years later, western peace activists try to prevent an American military bombardment of Baghdad by volunteering as human shields.

**A.D. 1995, Canada:** Twelve-year-old Craig Kielburger commits to changing the world after reading about the brutal murder of a child sold into slavery in Pakistan. He rallies his schoolmates and forms Free the Children – an NGO that fights for children's rights.

**A.D. 2009, Afghanistan:** A new law passes allowing husbands to withhold food from wives who don't obey their sexual demands.

**A.D. 2009, Canada:** Amnesty International raps the Canadian government for not protecting native women and girls. Over the summer, two Aboriginal friends are murdered in what could be a drugs-for-sex scandal.

## step eight

# GETTING
# HEARD

**A**rtists, storytellers, and cultural leaders in democratic socie-
ties can engage the soul and influence behavior more than
technology or government policy. When people hear a compel-
ling, intriguing, heartfelt story, they tend to connect with the
subject matter. Often, they identify with the situation and how
it can lead to change – more than if they're presented with statistics, diagrams, and cold hard facts. If your message is not getting
heard, look for the story. Ask yourself, "What's my story and how
can it change things?" Dramatic presentations, workshops, and
student-made videos are ways to be heard – just ask the kids of
Labrador who get their stories out every year at the Labrador
Creative Arts Festival.

A mound of winter coats, a tumble of boots, and steamed-up
windows mean a good turnout. The audience – locals from Goose
Bay and dozens of outlying communities – fills this makeshift
theater. From toddler to elder, they sit on hard stacking chairs,
lean against the walls, or jostle for position on the floor. The mike

crackles to life in Tim Borlase's hand, and a hush sweeps through the crowd. "Welcome to the 29th annual Labrador Creative Arts Festival." He pauses for wild applause, hoots, and whoops. "This year's theme is Global Soul Warming. How appropriate for this cold November night! Our first presentation is a short film brought to you by the student artists of Mushuau Innu Natuashish School. Please dim the lights for *How Others See Us*."

The soundless video opens with teenage boys forming a line in a school hallway. They're all wearing dark, hooded sweatshirts. Blazoned above the classroom door is a sign with five big white letters: I-G-L-O-O. The boys enter the classroom. The teacher signals for them to sit down, then hands out paper bags. He models how to effectively sniff gas. The students follow his instructions, sniff, sway, and then pass out. The film fades to black.

The lights come on. Everyone claps as a lineup of young men in dark hoodies walks onstage. Clear-eyed and serious, they take questions from the crowd.

"*Is it a good idea to show others how to sniff gas?*"

"Actually, the film doesn't teach that. You can't sniff gas that way, even if you want to. Besides, most people in our community have seen someone sniff gas. It's nothing new."

"*My question is, why did you use the word 'igloo' when Innu people use tents?*"

"That's pretty central to our theme. *You* know we use tents because you're from here. But other people lump us all together. Outsiders don't know that Métis, Innu, and Inuit are different peoples with different traditions."

Tim Borlase thanks the aspiring Innu actors and calls upon the drama club from Jens Haven Memorial School in Nain.

A girl steps to the front of the stage and announces, "Our play's called *Forever to Say Good-Bye*." Fiction based on fact, the drama club acts out the story of four teenagers coping with the sudden loss of a friend. They move through the many faces of grief – shock, anger, sadness, guilt, and despair. A fifth student plays the role of Life.

They're all survivors, drawing the audience into a dark world, trying to shed light onto a community shaken by suicide. There's no melodrama – they just tell it like it is. When the play ends, the applause is loud and long, without hoots and whoops.

Stepping out into the cold night, the theatergoers reflect on what they've just seen. Some of these students come from communities with the highest suicide rates in Canada. They've all experienced the loss of friends, neighbors, or family. They know how it feels to be left behind. And they know how to sniff gas. What can be done to change these young lives? At least now, the students know that they've been heard.

**STORY**

# *Being Heard at the Labrador Creative Arts Festival*

So, you're a teenager. What else is new? You probably have issues – acne, overbearing parents, school is boring, best friend's acting weird, you didn't make the team, or worse. Usually you can handle it – no big deal. But, add to these common teen problems living in a tiny isolated hamlet, where everyone knows your business but no one's listening. Then along comes a great opportunity – a dramatic one – that gives you a creative outlet.

In 1975, educator and drama specialist Tim Borlase helped launch the first Labrador Creative Arts Festival (LCAF). The goal was to provide students of Labrador communities with a means to explore their past and influence their future. Expressing themselves through performing and visual arts – storytelling, mime, dance, drumming, plays, writing – would celebrate their unique cultures and bring the students of Labrador together as a group. Borlase recognized the need for all students – but especially Métis, Innu, and Inuit children – to keep their traditions alive.

Over the years, student presentations have celebrated the good or exposed the bad – even the very bad. Each November at the LCAF, students air their concerns and address whatever is on their minds – as long as they approach their subject with honesty and integrity. Some students opt for lighthearted skits based on their own lives. The audience laughs as the awkward, shy boy asks a girl to dance; appreciates the mockery in a TV-survivor-show parody with a Labrador twist; or waits for the punch line in a clever retelling of a familiar folktale. The festival also provides a platform for addressing the "elephant in the room" – painful subjects that no one wants to talk about. There's always a range of subject matter, including abuse, date rape, self-esteem, accidental death of parents, or peer pressure. No matter what the focus, the students perform with intensity and heart.

For those with stage fright, the LCAF offers more than a theatrical debut. All week long, students choose from a variety of artistic experiences: making clay tiles that reflect their culture, learning drum dancing and putting on a show, engaging in a jazz jamming session, and making a community film, to name a few. After thirty-five years, the LCAF is Canada's longest-running children's festival, which endures because kids love it. Teachers and volunteers come and go, but a core group makes it happen. And it's always fresh.

Participation in the LCAF has proven to effect change in

individuals and their communities in unexpected ways.

- The students of Davis Inlet – an Innu community that was moved to Natuashish, Labrador, in December 2002 – were fed up and wanted better food, so they performed a play about the empty shelves in their general store. With politicians in the audience, federal planes soon arrived with provisions. Effective!
- In 2008, the local Inuit government band closed a uranium mine for a three-year environmental review. Postville teens wondered where they'd work when they finished high school. Would they be forced to move out of Labrador? They wrote and performed a play, directing their concerns to the Department of Mining and their own people, asking for a voice in community decisions.

## STRATEGIES

# *Use Theater/Be Heard*

Labrador is the Wild West of the province of Newfoundland and Labrador. About the size of New Zealand, it has a population of approximately 26,500 – the size of a small town elsewhere in the country. Vast distances and few roads separate many small communities. Despite the geography, people have connected through a long history of storytelling and theater. Archaeologists have found evidence of amphitheaters from over a thousand years ago. The Labrador Creative Arts Festival has built on this ancient theatrical tradition, starting with ninety participants in 1975 to over four thousand in 2008. Its growth has been organic in nature, responding and expanding to meet the needs of the students. If you want to replicate the LCAF in your community or school, here's how to get started, but beware! There will be growing pains. This well-oiled machine works something like this:

- Teachers of grades four through twelve pay a small fee and sign up their classes as soon as school starts in the fall.
- Students break into groups and craft their own forty-five-minute presentations. Sometimes one group writes and another group acts. All kids are encouraged to participate.
- Teachers provide support and guidance. Grandparents, parents, and older siblings volunteer too.
- Rehearsals happen before and after school, at lunch, and on weekends.
- Props and costumes are scrounged or made at little or no expense.
- Screenings and/or dress rehearsals help students polish their work.
- After two months of preparation and rehearsal, it's festival time. Students from as many schools as possible travel to Goose Bay, having raised funds in their home communities through bake sales, dances, etc.
- Professional artists (writers, broadcasters, musicians, dancers, painters, historians, clowns, etc.) from across Canada and the United States also converge on Goose Bay.
- Volunteers, many of whom were student or teacher participants in previous years, billet visiting students and artists, making this a truly intergenerational experience.
- During the school day, students and visiting artists act, sing, draw, write, and share their talents.
- Every night throughout the festival is theater night – plays

are performed in front of an audience that includes the other participants as well as the general public.

- One mentor is designated as the "animator" and leads group discussions following each presentation. Performers, students, and the audience at-large comment and ask questions.
- Labrador hospitality rounds out the event. It could include a potlatch – a supper with partridgeberry tea, *nikku* (dried caribou meat), and *pitsik* (arctic char); a night of rowdy, stomping, fiddle music; or a surprise visit from a group of mummers wearing wild costumes, their faces covered in masks. Local businesses often donate or sell the food at cost.
- For those schools that can't make the trip to Goose Bay, their communities host visiting artists so the effects of the festival are felt all around the region.
- Each year, the scripts are published in a binder and archived at the festival office to preserve them and to inspire future participants.

## Create a Logo – The LCAF Button Contest

A well-designed symbol beams out information in the blink of an eye: Panda = WWF; Mobius loop = recycling; red slash through a wineglass and dangling keys = Mothers Against Drunk Driving. Symbols trigger memory and remind people of the messages they convey. They ask for commitment or change in behavior: care about wildlife, recycle, don't drink and drive. You get the idea.

In keeping with the evolving nature of the LCAF, their symbol changes every year with a button-design contest. Students from all over Labrador submit their designs to the committee – each one unique. When one is chosen as the motif for the year, buttons are produced and given to all festival attendees.

When participants pin a button on their lapels at the end of the festival, they are paying tribute to a fantastic week of performing and watching theater, taking workshops, absorbing new ideas from visiting artists, making new friends, and renewing old acquaintances. The buttons symbolize their individual and their collective creativity and are tokens of hope: hope that their message has been heard and that they'll come back next year.

# Keeping Squeaky-Clean

Is the answer *a*, *b*, or *both a and b*? Michael Phelps is *a*) a superstar American swimmer who won eight Olympic gold medals *b*) a college student caught sucking an illegal substance from a bong? If you answered *both a and b*, you are correct. And, yes, what was he thinking?

You may not be the International Committee of the Red Cross or Save the Children. You may just be doing something local – for a park, a school, or a family. But what you're doing is important, and doing it ethically and responsibly is essential. Anyone with a Facebook account or a clip on YouTube knows you have no control over how quickly and widely information can travel. If you get involved in an organization, do your part to keep out of the gossip columns. Even a motherhood and apple-pie, community-supported group like the LCAF has to keep squeaky-clean. Cover your bases so that you can't be unfairly discredited.

- Keep meticulous financial records. If you receive money for your cause, open a separate bank account. Keep digital or journal records of month-to-month deposits and withdrawals.

- Keep all receipts for incidental expenses, such as postage or computer supplies.
- Start a scrapbook of any media coverage.
- Start a journal of your connection to your cause. Keep track of your concerns, small victories, and plans for the future.
- Make these records available to other interested students. They could advocate for you or replicate what you're doing in another school or community.

## *The Medium for the Message*

The Labrador Creative Arts Festival features drama. But there are lots of other creative ways to get attention. Whether it's attracting a small crowd around a soapbox or beaming a concert into millions of homes by satellite, one way to get heard is to gather people round.

**A.D. 1862, Belgium:** Victor Hugo, banished by Napoléon, publishes *Les Misérables* from exile. At the time, the book is banned in France, but the story continues to draw attention to the pain of revolution and the plight of the poor in a popular musical of the same name.

**A.D. 1872, England:** The saying "He's on his soapbox" is first used for off-the-cuff public speaking while standing on a box. Hyde Park, in downtown London, has a designated Speakers' Corner, where soapboxers continue to give Sunday orations.

**A.D. 1901, United States:** The statement "We Shall Overcome" appears in a gospel hymn written by Reverend

Charles Tindley. In the 1960s, it's written into the rallying anthem for the African-American Civil Rights Movement.

**A.D. 1933, United States:** Franklin D. Roosevelt gives his first of thirty "fireside chats" over the radio. In a friendly and down-to-earth manner, he explains his government's stand on key issues of the day – from the Bank Crisis and the New Deal to the Great Depression and World War II – over the next eleven years.

**A.D. 1969, Canada:** Beatle John Lennon records "Give Peace a Chance" on June 1st from a Montreal hotel room while he and his bride, Yoko Ono, stage a "bed-in" to promote peace. The song becomes an anthem of the American Anti-War Movement.

**A.D. 1970, United States:** Days after four students die during anti-war demonstrations at Kent State University, singer Neil Young pens the protest song "Ohio." Recorded and released within a month, the lyrics directly blame President Richard Nixon for the tragedy.

**A.D. 1985, England**: Musicians Bob Geldof and Midge Ure coordinate a simultaneous, multicity charity concert on July 13, seen worldwide via satellite television, with about 400 million people in sixty countries watching live. Viewers call in donations for famine relief in Ethiopia, with a final tally of about 150 million British pounds.

**A.D. 1987, United States:** The first square of the AIDS Memorial Quilt is sewn to remember the life of Marvin Feldman. Now there are 46,000 3 x 6 squares – a powerful reminder of lives lost to HIV.

**A.D. 1989, China:** Students from the Central Academy of Fine Arts unveil their sculpture called the *Goddess of Democracy* in Tiananmen Square to shouts of "Long live democracy." Five days later, government soldiers destroy it in the assault that ends the democracy movement.

**A.D. 1989, Germany:** The Berlin Wall, a physical and symbolic divide between democratic and communist Germany, becomes a rallying point for thousands of pro-democracy demonstrators. They gradually tear it down, using hammers, mallets, heavy equipment, and their bare hands.

**A.D. 2005, United States:** *Time* magazine names screenwriter Michael Moore one of the world's one hundred most influential people. His film *Bowling for Columbine* demands America look to its soul and questions why individuals can own assault weapons.

**A.D. 2006, Canada:** Filmed in China and Bangladesh, the movie *Manufactured Landscapes*, which premieres at the Toronto Film Festival, explores globalization. With breathtaking cinematography and limited commentary, photographer Edward Burtynsky makes a clear connection between consumerism and pollution.

**A.D. 2009, United States:** President Barack Obama reacts to the death of Senator Edward Kennedy and pays tribute to the changes Kennedy effected in his country: "For five decades, virtually every major piece of legislation to advance the civil rights, health, and economic well-being of the American people bore his name and resulted from his efforts."

# LIFE
# AFTER
# CHANGE

Spending his early years in Nigeria, Kayode Fatoba didn't understand why there was such a gap between the rich and the poor. He dreamt of a world where everyone had enough.

Moving to Toronto at the age of ten blew those dreams out of the water. His neighborhood had the worst possible reputation – people said nothing good ever came from there. One day, Kayode met a cool athletic kid who skipped school to shoot hoops. All the other kids looked up to this guy, and some even cut class to watch him practice. The buzz was, he'd land a scholarship in the United States with a shot at the big show – the NBA. But, around the court, when the older kids got bored, they picked on the younger ones and videoed fights to post on YouTube. Kayode wondered how truancy, bullying, and violence could end in a scholarship. There had to be a better way. He decided that by passively watching from the sidelines, he was accepting what people said about his neighborhood. So, believing in the possibility of change, he took charge of his life and decided to pursue *his* game of choice – soccer. This conscious choice made the difference for Kayode Fatoba and for dozens of aspiring young soccer players in his community.

Kayode's first break came when his high-school teacher selected him for a leadership camp run by the city. For one week, Kayode and other top students, passionate for sports, were groomed as leaders and trained in coaching. Armed with referee and coaching certificates, Kayode headed straight for the basketball court. He asked the hangers-on if they wanted to play a sport for themselves or watch the NBA wannabe. How about soccer? Three kids – ages twelve, thirteen, and fifteen – turned up for his first practice. They had no jerseys, cleats, shin pads, or socks. The twelve-year-old bristled with attitude and had a reputation as a notorious hood. Kayode quickly learned that becoming an amateur psychologist was part of being coach. He started with soccer stunts and tricks, hoping he'd gain the boys' confidence and trust while making soccer fun. Soon he was up to seven players.

After losing their first three local league games, Kayode signed the team up for a soccer banquet held outside the neighborhood. In borrowed dress clothes and with proud mothers photographing their departure, the ragtag team was shown that there was "water outside the desert." There they met accomplished soccer players and respected business types, returning with a new outlook and broader goals. When Kayode shouted, "Run laps!" there was no back talk or laziness. This team was going places.

Kayode's daily routine became a juggling act. With at least four balls in the air – school, practice, part-time job, and homework – he sometimes felt he was struggling alone. Uniforms and equipment cost money, so he used his own savings. Then he suggested the team try fundraising. Some players raised cash while others spent the money they collected on themselves. They desperately needed a sponsor, but everyone Kayode asked was skeptical. Finally a hot-dog vendor, new to the neighborhood, took an interest. He saw Kayode herding his team – eleven kids now – to the park for practice and tagged along. Not only did the hot-dog man pay for registration and equipment, he gave the kids free food, especially when they won their games.

During the second season, Kayode raised the bar for his growing team of twenty-five players. He made good grades a prerequisite for participation and kept tabs on how they were doing at school. Players learned that he meant business, benching those who were under-performing in life outside soccer. Some kids, including one of his first recruits, had turned into what Kayode termed "sick" soccer players, meaning, they were good! The whole team now recognized the positive influence the soccer program was having on their community.

Kayode's leadership skills brought him another break. He won a full scholarship from a national bank, which sent him off to university.

Kayode has completed his first year of science and is on his way to fulfilling his next dream: to become a medical doctor. His soccer program now attracts over eighty kids that play organized and scheduled games. And he's grooming some of his best players as leaders and coaches. As soon as they're game ready, Kayode will kick them a forward pass and let them carry the ball.

# The Right to Play: The Ins and Outs of International Volunteerism

Paco Barnett started playing soccer when he was six. From the age of twelve on, he belonged to at least three soccer teams at any given time. School mattered too, of course, but his world revolved around a perfectly spherical leather ball. When the time came for university, he double-majored in kinesiology (the study of human movement) and French (because he's Canadian, eh?) while playing soccer for his university team, the Mustangs.

Loving sport and being physically active was at the heart of Paco's education. In a lecture hall one autumn afternoon, the guest speaker was from an organization called Right to Play (RTP). Johann Koss – a many-medaled Norwegian Olympic athlete, medical doctor, MBA holder, and now the leader of RTP – spoke passionately about harnessing the power of sport and using it for the bigger purpose of helping humanity. Paco was blown away by the possibilities. For him, this was the ultimate combination – sport as a means of helping people. He buckled down and finished his degree, keeping Koss's message in the back of his mind.

Fast-forward three years and find Paco, a freshly-minted international volunteer, catapulted into the Tanzanian village of Mugumu, which means "difficult place" in Swahili. Little more than a truck stop, it's smack in the middle of the Serengeti Plain, two hours from Lake Victoria. Paco hit the ground running, pumped, and ready to establish a soccer program for about eight thousand kids. In one year. Wow! He'd have to contact local officials and wade through a foreign culture while studying Swahili 101 on the fly. Plus he'd eat, sleep, and do laundry in a village without running water, electricity, phones, Internet, or refrigeration, not to mention his wild neighbors, including lions, elephants, black mambas, hippos, and Cape buffalo. Parked out front of his house was Right to Play's spanking new four-wheel-drive truck – the single most valuable item in the village. Was he safe? Was he crazy to be here?

The "I can do it all" switch went off in Paco's brain, and "I can't do anything" flashed brightly. But not for long. Armed with the power of positive thinking, he bumbled through the early weeks, making mistakes and plunging ahead. He learned that dealing with bureaucrats took time and that he'd better respect the pecking order. When the district commissioner was out of town for two weeks, Paco assumed his subordinate had authority. Not so! He gave a RTP T-shirt to the wrong person, trod on a few toes, and finally got the green light. But he'd learned something valuable – green means "go slow."

Paco recruited community helpers, found translators, and devoted four months to laying the groundwork so the project would get up and running and be sustainable. There were hurdles he refused to jump – such as bribing government officials – but he did avoid jail by paying a ten-dollar speeding ticket.

An obvious avenue for introducing organized sport was through the existing school system. Most Tanzanian kids attend school regularly. After many visits to principals and teaching staff, taking care to respect local customs, Paco drew up contracts with eight schools. These established what RTP would provide and each school's commitment in return. Paco helped launch regular physical-education regimes that complemented the existing curriculums and provided coach-training to any interested teacher. He held seminars to highlight the connection between sport, play, and learning. Coaches-in-training realized that sport could provide life lessons, such as conflict resolution. Kids were encouraged to deconstruct how they felt after a rousing game of soccer. Did it help them mentally? Was it fun? Did they feel part of the team?

With new skills, tools, and programming, coaches still faced the challenge of introducing something totally untried to large groups of kids. And then Paco introduced another concept – he encouraged older students to supervise and run the games.

Keeping it simple and low-budget meant sweet-talking companies working nearby into using their heavy earth-moving equipment to level off playing fields. Paco and the children made soccer balls from scrap plastic bags tied with string. Smaller ones were crafted for little kids and up to regulation size for the older ones. Once the schools had the sport programs up and running, RTP brought in Frisbees, pylons, and hula hoops to diversify the games.

During his year in Tanzania, Paco had good days and bad days. Sometimes he'd be on the road for twelve dusty hours and arrive at a school to find that playing sports was temporarily suspended. He'd wonder why he was bothering – wasting time and money. Then he'd have what he called a WOW day, such as the time he wheeled into a schoolyard to find five hundred kids playing soccer, with cheering coaches and grinning parents. The principal would take him by the hand in a gesture of friendship, and they'd walk and talk. One principal said, "Ever since we started running these programs, a lot more children are coming to school." Paco was stunned; the principal was not surprised. WOW! He had the best job in the world that day.

Off-hours were tough. Paco's family, girlfriend, and friends were thousands of miles away – it was lonely. He couldn't even go out for a walk by himself because of predators, humans included. And reading after dark meant squinting beside a smoky kerosene lantern.

Then it was time to go home. How could Paco abandon the project? Would he ever see these wonderful people again? He left feeling guilty for his privileged life in the West. Stopping at the grocery store with his dad on the way home from the airport nearly made him sick. The choices and colors dazzled as he remembered the tomato vendor in Mugumu, sitting on the ground ready to barter, or the celebratory wildebeest barbecue for the entire village during the migration season.

Two and a half years later, the RTP sports program is thriving in the Mugumu region, with paid members of the community doing the job of international volunteers. Paco completed teachers college and is currently a French teacher and soccer coach in London, Ontario. He raised ten thousand dollars and went back to Tanzania in the summer of 2009 to build a library in a remote village, buying native construction materials and hiring local workers. You can be sure he took a few perfectly spherical leather soccer balls along in his luggage.

Right to Play is an example of an international organization that began with one individual. At the Lillehammer Olympics in Norway in 1994, Johann Olav Koss had been selected to fundraise by a cooperative group of NGOs for people affected by war and disaster. Koss rose to the challenge, then, over time, his efforts shifted direction and morphed into Right to Play, whose torch gets passed forward from one volunteer to another.

# Prepare to Participate: The Red Cross Story

Henry Dunant, a Swiss businessman traveling in Italy in 1859, came upon a gruesome scene – a battlefield littered with forty thousand dead, dying, and wounded soldiers left unattended by the dispersing French and Austrian armies. He galvanized into action, aided by neighboring villagers, and helped all the men he could, no matter which uniform they wore. His self-published eyewitness account laid the groundwork for the Geneva Conventions for humane treatment of combatants and for the founding of the International Committee of the Red Cross and the International Federation of the Red Crescent.

Dunant's "roll up your sleeves" attitude has been typical of Red Cross responses ever since. Starting with fair treatment of war combatants and prisoners, the Red Cross has continued to broaden its involvement and provide relief in cases of flood, mudslide, chemical spill, fire, hurricane, earthquake, landmines, tsunami, volcanic eruption, famine, train derailment, air disaster, terrorist attack, and so on. And it offers many ways to prepare yourself should your community need you to roll up your sleeves:

- *Cardiopulmonary resuscitation (CPR)* – There are seconds to respond if someone is drowning or collapses with a heart attack. Performing CPR can keep that person alive until professional help arrives.
- *First aid* – A Red Cross first-aid course teaches skills such as bandaging, stopping bleeding, and treating hypothermia. When someone is choking, know how to perform the Heimlich maneuver. If you're the one who can't breathe, learn the signal to get help.

- *Water safety and swimming lessons* – Red Cross certified swimming instruction helps prevent unnecessary tragedy. If you live near water, be a skilled swimmer.
- *Babysitting courses* – These involve a lot more than changing diapers. Learn how to prevent house fires, respond to accidental poisoning, and become a "temporary adult" when you're the oldest one around.
- *Leadership workshops* – Discover how to keep the peace, handle bullies, and avoid abuse.

Dunant's experience in Italy drove home the need for preparedness, which has been central to the ongoing success of the Red Cross. If you follow any disaster – large or small – you will notice that the Red Cross is often the first group on the scene, offering aid in the form of tents, water, food, and clothing. That's because it is constantly replenishing its supplies in order to be ready for the next emergency.

**SKILLS**

# *Measuring Personal Change*

Kayode, Paco, and volunteers of the Red Cross share something in common. They've offered help under difficult circumstances, made fantastic contributions, and, at some point, let others step into their shoes. They've all effected change and changed themselves in the process.

Kayode has learned it's not easy to practice what he preaches. His first year of university was harder than he expected, and now he'll have to pull up his average if he wants to get into medical school. He knows he's a role model for younger kids, so he doesn't want to disappoint them or himself. And, thinking ahead to next summer, he's applying for a grant to run a more structured soccer camp, with over eighty local boys and girls. He'll hire staff from his "sick" player pool, knowing he can't do it alone.

Paco no longer gives "obligatory" Christmas and birthday presents to his family and friends. Instead, he suggests doing an activity together, or, in the case of his aging grandparents, he offers his younger self for a day of chores. Compared to his friends in Mugumu, these people don't really need anything. And despite this new personal rule, Paco keeps on giving.

Paco will never forget his year in Tanzania, but he still recorded the experience by sending home a series of journal-like E-mails and by taking thousands of photos. He recorded day-to-day events and comments from people he met, sharing his frustrations as well as joys. Some of his action shots from WOW days on the soccer pitch belong on Discovery or in *National Geographic*. With these tools, he's well equipped to give motivating talks in schools. By sharing his experiences, he fires others up too. And Paco keeps his library-building project alive through updates on his blog.

Whether you want to share your experiences or keep them private, the routine of keeping a journal or diary will help you deconstruct what you've accomplished, show you if and where you've gone wrong, and track your contributions. Here's what helps:

- Establish a routine of writing – morning, evening, daily, weekly – you choose. Unless you set aside the time, you might start but not continue.
- Tell the facts, but include your feelings and reflections too.
- Remember: the more detail the better. You might use your

journal as the basis for an A+ essay or a magazine article in the future.

- If you see that you are whining, it may be time to take a break. Volunteers need to refuel themselves, just like anyone who is working hard!
- If you have a camera, take photos every step of the way.
- Whether your journal is paper or paperless, store it safely for posterity. Send yourself a backup E-mail once a week.

**TIMELINE** *MILESTONES AND SETBACKS*

# Games for Change

From the Olympic stadiums of Greece to soccer pitches in modern-day Tanzania, sport has served a higher purpose than play. It has brightened dark days, played a positive role in times of war, and been a vehicle to reach out to disadvantaged or injured kids. If you're an athlete, your game could mean change.

**776 B.C., Greece:** The earliest Olympic Games feature running competitions among male athletes from Greek city-states. A general truce suspends all wars before and during the games, so that athletes and spectators can attend safely.

**264 B.C., Italy:** Three pairs of skilled gladiators, thought to be Roman slaves, fight to the death as entertainment at the funeral of leader Brutus Pera. Gladiator matches eventually become popular, showcasing military agility, honor, and prowess. But the games degrade into brutal, bloody spectacles until they are banned, about seven hundred years later.

**A.D. 1292, England:** Edward I's Statute of Arms for Tournaments regulates popular jousting melees to reduce bloodshed. The ideal of chivalry catches on, requiring knights to abide by rules of fair play and to champion fair ladies.

**A.D. 1896, Greece:** The modern Olympic Games begin, spearheaded by Baron Pierre de Coubertin. His philosophy is to stage competitions every four years to promote physical fitness and internationalism.

**A.D. 1948, Europe:** The International Military Sports Council is founded to promote friendship and peace off the battlefield. With 131 member countries, soldiers can participate in over twenty sporting events annually – including the Military World Games – featuring soccer, running, golf, and volleyball.

**A.D. 1964, Japan:** South Africa is excluded from the Olympic Games because of its policy of racial discrimination in sport and competition. The boycott of apartheid sports spreads and is not lifted until the apartheid laws are repealed in 1991.

**A.D. 1970, Canada:** Yellowknife, NWT, hosts the first Arctic Winter Games, bringing together athletes from all over the north, around the globe. Held every other year, the games brighten the dark winter days as athletes share talents, stories, meals, and friendships.

**A.D. 1972, Canada:** The Cold War thaws briefly as Canada and Russia play an eight-game hockey series. Paul Henderson, who scores the winning goal for Canada, uses his fame to help others. One of his signed jerseys is auctioned for about five thousand dollars, raising money for charity.

**A.D. 1972, Germany:** Militant terrorists calling themselves Black September take hostages and murder eleven Israeli national-team athletes and coaches at the Munich Olympics. The games are suspended for a memorial service and then reconvene.

**A.D. 1972, *United States:*** Pittsburgh Pirates right fielder and off-season charity worker Roberto Clemente dies when the plane he charters to take relief supplies to Nicaraguan earthquake victims crashes after takeoff. Since then, Major League Baseball annually presents the Roberto Clemente Award to a player selected for both humanitarian and on-field performance.

**A.D. 1980, *Russia:*** Over sixty countries refuse to participate in the Olympic Games in Moscow to protest against the Russian invasion of Afghanistan. In retaliation, Russian and fourteen Eastern Bloc allies boycott the Los Angeles Olympics four years later.

**A.D. 1996, *United States:*** Retired boxer Muhammed Ali lights the Olympic flame in Atlanta, Georgia. Ali's humanitarian work later earns him the designation United Nations Messenger of Peace as well as the Presidential Medal of Freedom.

**A.D. 2001, *United States:*** Basketball superstar Shaquille O'Neal pledges $1 million to the Boys and Girls Clubs of America.

**A.D. 2007, *United States:*** The world's number-one female golfer, Annika Sorenstam, becomes an ambassador for Make-A-Wish, a foundation that grants wishes for children with life-threatening medical conditions.

# YOUR CHANCE TO
# BE THE CHANGE

**Y**ou're sitting in the school lunchroom with friends, throwing around ideas about where you'll put your energy to really make a difference.

One friend is focused on improving accessibility for disabled kids – not just obvious things like adding wheelchair ramps, but determining ways they can be included in everything. Several are committed to forwarding the rights and education of young women, especially in third-world countries. One girl organizes a school-sponsored fast day every year to raise awareness and money for world hunger. She has new ideas this time. Two others are interested in ecological and carbon footprints – they think a footprint is a great image for human environmental impact. "If only there was something as easy as a recycling box for energy conservation," one of them says, "we could beat global warming."

With that, you all look at the recycling area in the lunchroom just in time to see the caretaker dump the paper, pop cans, compost, and plastic recycling containers into his big garbage bin.

Amazed, you watch him trash all the sorted recycling by putting it into the regular garbage.

## Step 1 – I'm Fed Up

You're stunned, but your footprint friends are furious. "Look at that!" one of them calls out. "No one cares, even when the recycling containers are right there." The other groans, "We'll never beat climate change!"

A couple of you approach the caretaker and ask why he's pitching everything to landfill. He explains, "You kids throw garbage in with the recyclables. I don't have time or inclination to pick through your contaminated mess."

You spot used tissues, apple cores, smashed glass, soiled wooden skewers, smeared plastic wrap, part of a broken chair, and other grossness mixed in with the recyclables and can't blame him. When the caretaker mutters, "Stupid waste of energy," you think he means *his* energy, and then you realize he means energy as in fuel and electricity because he continues: "Recycling material near home is far more efficient than trucking natural resources from the wilderness." So, the caretaker is thinking "footprint" too.

Back at the lunch table, you all agree that it's your fellow students that contaminate the recycling. Disinterested, lazy, thoughtless, hurried, whatever! Someone says, "Look, we all slip up. So, what are we going to do about it?"

## Step 2 – What's Wrong?

The girl with a deep concern for world hunger says, "I always thought that recycling was about waste, not energy."

Another says, "Actually, there are three more 'r's' – reduce, reuse, and refuse. Don't forget 'refuse.'"

One friend remembers calculating in class, "Making a new

aluminum can from recycled aluminum – rather than ore fresh from a mine – saves enough energy for someone to play *three* hours of video games. But reusing a glass bottle – including collecting, washing, refilling, rather than making one from scratch – saves enough energy to play *four*."

A younger kid joins the group and comments irritatingly on every idea. No one stops him.

After much banter, you all agree that cool facts could be used in a campaign to interest everyone in recycling. Volunteers offer to spend part of the evening digging up information.

One friend offers, "I'll use my computer to design new graphics to post over the different bins to make it clear what's supposed to go into each one."

The talkative younger kid blurts, "I'll make a giant papier-mâché blue whale to hang over the whole recycling area," and everyone rolls their eyes.

As you break up for class, you pass the caretaker in the hall. You tell him you are going to solve this. He says, "Keep me in the loop – I'd like to help."

### Step Three – Great Minds Think Alike

Next day, you're all together again in the lunchroom.

The graphic designer passes around her work. She has used the generic, traditional symbols for paper and cans and so on, but jazzed them up with color. She also used the words WE RECYCLE on every container. "Not my idea," she says, "but a good one."

The fact collectors have dug up great information, and you spend a lot of time thinking about the best way to use it. The "blue whale kid" makes lots of remarks, but doesn't mention his hanging sculpture. The activity at your table attracts attention, and others stop to listen. A few sit down to join the discussion.

Maybe because you still have the graphics of the recycling symbols on the table, you are all thinking about communicating with posters. Then someone suggests, "We can ask the principal about speaking over the intercom at announcements, on a regular basis, as well as come up with visual messages."

Lots of ideas, lots of energy. You talk about trying to involve the whole school in making a behavior change. You say, "This is good. The bigger our team is to start, the fewer people we have to convince!"

## Step Four – Good Plans, Good Luck

Next lunch, most of you meet again. Ideas come so fast that someone with a laptop takes notes.

As you recap, the caretaker stops by and listens. The neat new graphic signs above the recycling bins are falling off the wall, and he offers a good adhesive to hold cardboard on block cement.

Someone comes up with the idea of doing a weigh-in of total garbage one day a week for several months, recording improvements on a giant wall garbage-o-meter. The caretaker offers a cupboard to keep any pieces of equipment, but thinks you'll need to talk to the physics department about borrowing a small block and tackle.

The campaign to improve the school's environmental impact is sorting itself into subgroups – those organizing the weigh-in, hall posters, and announcements. Everyone who wants to get involved has something to do, even though nothing has really been done yet.

## Step Five – Baby Steps, Giant Leaps

Next day begins with a few downers. Exam time approaches, and your group is smaller in size. And the garbage and recycling area is a bigger mess than usual.

Every subgroup has done a little preparation, but it all seems a bit overwhelming.

Then someone has a good idea: "Let's sort the campaign messages like sorting waste – start off with paper, a week later cans, and then different grades of plastic. Add the weigh-in towards the end, and run it for several more weeks with a footprint theme."

Suddenly it all seems more doable. You divvy up the work and set a date-and-time goal for blitzing facts, posters, and announcements – starting with paper use and recycling.

The "blue whale kid" says, "I need to talk to the caretaker about hooks in the ceiling." It seems so off-topic.

### Step Six – Butting Heads

Your initial campaign works well. After several weeks, everyone feels good about it.

But then you walk into the lunchroom and find the graphic symbols spoiled with graffiti and the words "garbage police" scribbled everywhere. Mustard and ketchup – or something equally goopey – are sprayed all over the recycling area. Globs of wet toilet paper are everywhere too. No one has any idea who did it or when.

The caretaker is angry; so is the principal. It feels like their anger is directed at you. The subgroup responsible for announcements say they quit – it's not worth their time. One of your team shouts at a little kid who throws a pop can in with the compost. The kid shouts back, "I can do what I want!"

Good intentions are unraveling.

### Step Seven – When the Going Gets Tough, the Tough Get Going

Walking home from school with a friend, neither of you wants to talk it through. You'd like to be doing something for yourselves.

All sorts of things go through your mind. You remember that this started out because it was so infuriating that your peers weren't even bothering to recycle when it was all set up to be easy to do. Why should they bother?

Then, for whatever reason, a small part of you resolves not to give in. You decide you're going to be upbeat about this. You refuse to abandon your ideals or give up on people.

You and your friend practice positive one-liners in response to each other's invented taunts. Slowly, your energy returns.

## Step Eight – Getting Heard

So, you call a meeting of the team – same place, regular time. You talk about your "be-positive" strategy. You have to walk some kids through it – one friend walks out. In the end, the rest of you decide to carry on with the plan, the next step being the garbage weigh-in.

The group decides to start with a skit to grab attention. You brainstorm ideas for plot and recycled costumes. Someone gets all excited about phone messaging to advertise the skit, demonstrating how few degrees of separation we are. You don't really understand what they mean, but figure if they're really into it, others will be too. The energy is back, and the weigh-in moves forward.

Then the caretaker and the "blue whale kid" come in, carrying a huge, long, elegant, handmade papier mâché sculpture, which they hang on hooks over the recycling area. It is awesome. And, finally, you all get it: making the effort to recycle waste helps endangered animals and helps Earth.

## Step Nine – Life After Change

When all is said and done, your campaign has been a hit. The caretaker now sends on the sorted recycling most days. He calls it "a measure of success."

You learned a lot about what worked and what didn't. Teaming up with friends, setting doable goals, and keeping positive were keys to success. You learned that the word "should" doesn't help.

As summer approaches, the caretaker points out that, next fall, a whole new contingent of students will be entering the school. There may be new materials to sort out of garbage, and the new students will have to be brought up to speed. But you have the summer to think about how to sustain the success already achieved. And you have options for the future, with a strong group behind you and new like-minded kids coming aboard.

# The Recycling Blue Box Story

Will that be paper, glass, plastic, metal, organics, or garbage? Thirty years ago, just about the only choice was garbage. How did such big change happen?

In the 1960s and 1970s, cities and towns faced more and more garbage – and bulging landfills. New landfills cost taxpayers money, and nobody wanted one next door because, despite all the technological improvements, landfills still featured rats, seagulls, blowing trash, and lineups of stinky garbage trucks. NIMBY-ism (the Not In My Back Yard syndrome) spread through many communities, so that finding good sites for landfills got harder and harder.

Some people looked over all that garbage and spotted reusable items. They thought, *Couldn't household waste be mined for fiber and materials right in cities? Surely collecting metal, glass, and paper in towns was more efficient than traveling far afield to look for,*

124

*extract, process, and ship virgin materials into cities?* Some keeners set up community depots, where families could bring their sorted waste – cans, bottles, and newspapers. When these urban miners had stockpiled enough, they sold the recovered materials to industry. That helped pay for the service they offered. It took a lot of scrambling to find markets for the metals and fibers, but recycling-depot folks were truly committed. As the economic and environmental sense behind recycling sank in, some towns tested curbside recycling programs, including the Canadian military base at Camp Borden.

Meanwhile, in Ontario, Canada, Pollution Probe dramatized the issue of recycling with theatrical stunts. In 1975, Probers traveled around the province with a coffin, asking the public to fill it with nickel coins. Once full, the coffin was given to the premier with the request that he "bury the pop can" and regulate all soft-drink companies to place their product in returnable glass bottles. Later, a Prober named Tony Barrett challenged the Minister of the Environment to a public wager called the "Great Garbage Gamble." Tony would donate one hundred dollars to a university environmental-studies award for every cabinet minister who effectively recycled at home; the environment minister would donate the same amount for every minister who didn't. The press loved the story, reporting on it regularly, and thereby increasing the public interest in recycling.

Then, in 1981, Nyle Ludolph, a recycling enthusiast, teamed up with the group that had piloted the project at Camp Borden and brought other communications and recycling experts on board. They persuaded the company Nyle worked for – Laidlaw Waste Systems Ltd. of Kitchener – to run a large-scale curbside project. It was a win-win partnership.

Drawing on their combined experience, the partners created a smart marketing plan. They came up with slogans – "You Can Make a Difference" and "We Recycle." They used a stylized Mobius loop as a symbol on collection trucks, bins, and communications. Manufacturers stamped the same symbol on their packaging. Nyle Ludolph and his partners created generic graphics for newspapers, glass bottles, and cans that helped people sort. They created user-friendly brochures to explain the urgent need to recycle household waste and how to do it. They found markets for recovered fiber and material – *aka* recycled stuff. And the partners designed a box for householders to fill, until it was time to take the recycling to the curb for regular, garbage-day pickup. They chose the color blue for the box. Why blue? No one remembers exactly, but it was a great choice. When the pilot project ran in parts of Kitchener, Ontario, residents who were near recycling areas – but not part of the test – requested the opportunity to participate. It turned out that the box itself was so appealing and visible, everybody noticed! People who forgot when it was recycling day only had to look up and down their street to be reminded to put out their recycling. And people who didn't have the service saw how easy it was and asked for it! The partnership knew it had found a winner.

Despite its success, Laidlaw Waste Systems Ltd. nearly lost the next tender for garbage collection in the city. Another company, with no interest in recycling, underbid Laidlaw by about four hundred thousand dollars. City Council almost gave it the contract, but was won over to recycling by a presentation from Pollution Probe and by four grade-three students who read a poem they wrote about recycling to the meeting. One of their lines was "We need to keep recycling so vote for the blue bin."

Then Coca-Cola and other soft-drink manufacturers moved to package their product in plastic bottles and aluminum cans with zip tops. Reusable, deposit-paid glass bottles were on their way out. Environmentalists recognized how recyclable aluminum was – a can could be turned back into another can and be on the shelf with fresh pop inside within six weeks, if properly recycled. The soft-drink giants agreed to help finance household recycling if they could market their pop in the new containers.

Eventually, curbside recycling systems spread to communities around the world. As the idea caught on, increased markets for recycled materials opened up, and more kinds of household waste joined the recycling stream. Recycling spread from homes to businesses to lunchrooms. Special trucks were designed to collect it all. Cities and towns got a break on their big landfill costs, but not a free ride.

As more communities participated in recycling and added their ideas, the system improved. User-friendly websites now help families with their questions about what's recyclable. Bins on wheels replace blue boxes in communities where households are so efficient at recycling – and choosing to buy products that are recyclable – that small boxes no longer hold enough! Marketers have studied who in households are most committed to recycling so they can gear their communications to them. It turns out women and kids are the most consistent recyclers, with teenagers and apartment-dwellers being the least. Men take the most interest in recycling computers and other electronics.

Today, household curbside recycling is taken for granted in many large communities. In fact, it's hard to imagine a time when recycling wasn't an ordinary, everyday process. The blue box is a symbol of how people can change – in awareness, care, and habits. But many cities have yet to pitch in. . . .

# Future Steps

When your project is winding down and you're ready for another challenge, take a moment. . . . Evaluate what steps went well and why. Would you do things the same way again? Identify the steps you tripped on, and determine what you would avoid or improve on for future projects or causes.

### Step One: I'm Fed Up
☐ I was negative for too long.
☐ I was able to turn my negativity into positive action.
☐ Next time, I will recognize the symptoms of being fed up earlier, so I can turn it into positive action faster.
☐ Determining my ethical self-portrait was helpful.
This step went well because _____
Next time, I will _____

### Step Two: What's Wrong?
☐ It took me a long time to define the issue.
☐ I knew what was wrong, but found the issue hard to research.
☐ Describing the heart of the issue for others was harder than identifying it or researching it.
☐ Composing a brief (summary) was constructive.
This step went well because _____
Next time, I will _____

### Step Three: Great Minds Think Alike
☐ I had problems identifying/finding partners and/or supporters.
☐ I was able to work well with partners and/or supporters.
☐ I was able to get the opposition to listen to my cause. I even won over some doubters.

128

☐ I was able to organize and participate in a meeting to move the cause forward.

This step went well because _____

Next time, I will _____

## Step Four: Good Plans, Good Luck

☐ I had some lucky breaks, but would have been able to use them better if I'd been more prepared.

☐ I planned ahead and was able to take advantage of some good opportunities.

☐ Planning, not luck, accounted for all the successes I had.

☐ Preparing for a media interview was helpful.

This step went well because _____

Next time, I will _____

## Step Five: Baby Steps, Giant Leaps

☐ It was difficult to break my issue down into small, attainable goals.

☐ I was able to break down the issue into small, attainable goals and reach for them one at a time.

☐ I went for my ultimate goal from the start.

☐ Creating visual appeal (poster/posting) for my issue was helpful.

This step went well because _____

Next time, I will _____

## Step Six: Butting Heads

☐ I achieved my goals without having to deal with a power struggle.

☐ I faced a power struggle with significant confrontation and found it exhausting.

☐ I faced a power struggle with significant confrontation, but found that working through it was the turning point in achieving my goals.

☐ Identifying manipulative devices was helpful in dealing with confrontations and power struggles.

This step went well because _____

Next time, I will _____

## Step Seven: When the Going Gets Tough, the Tough Get Going

☐ I experienced a major low point, where all seemed hopeless, before reaching my goals.

☐ I can put my finger on something personal that helped me turn around what seemed to be a hopeless effort.

☐ I was able to translate my personal commitment into something that inspired others to help me.

☐ The information on fundraising was helpful in attracting supporters as well as in achieving my goals.

This step went well because _____

Next time, I will _____

## Step Eight: Getting Heard

☐ I found that my cause got mired in red tape/apathy/disinterest, and I cast around for a way to bring it back to life.

☐ I used the arts – music, drama, visual arts – as a way to express the change I sought.

☐ I found that a dramatic expression of my cause was the turning point to success.

☐ Keeping records, particularly financial records, turned out to be an important strategy in supporting the credibility of my cause.

This step went well because _____

Next time, I will _____

## Step Nine: Life After Change

☐ There came a point when I felt it was time to move on.

☐ I was able to pave the way for a smooth transition for my leaving the project.

☐ The cause continues well now, after my participation.

☐ I found that reflecting on the project through a journal was helpful.

This step went well because _____

Next time, I will _____

☐ This evaluation has been useful.

**TIMELINE** *MILESTONES AND SETBACKS*

# Climate Change

As an activist, how would you deal with waste causing the greenhouse effect, climate change, or global warming? Recycling helps slow down climate change because it's more energy-efficient than extracting and transporting virgin raw materials. But we have to do more than recycle to turn down the global thermostat. We have to cut back on waste in the form of exhaust from our cars, furnaces, air conditioners, etc. Carbon dioxide ($CO_2$) is waste when it's a by-product of burning fossil fuels. And there is a limit to the amount of $CO_2$ that Earth can absorb. If we could come up with an easy way to reduce our $CO_2$ waste, it would lead to a healthier planet.

**A.D. 1784, Scotland:** James Watt patents the steam locomotive. His improvements to the steam engine jump-start the Industrial Revolution – a new age that consumes huge volumes of fossil fuel, produces severe air pollution, releases clouds of $CO_2$ into the atmosphere, and eventually triggers human-induced global warming.

**A.D. 1824, France:** Jean Baptiste Joseph Fourier describes how Earth's atmosphere traps the sun's heat like a giant glass jar – the first scientific explanation to what becomes known as the greenhouse effect.

**A.D. 1908, Sweden:** Scientist Svante Arrhenius predicts that continued burning of coal and oil will cause global warming. He suggests that a five-degree increase in temperature, resulting from a doubling of atmospheric $CO_2$, will be beneficial for humans.

**A.D. 1957, United States:** Roger Revelle of the Scripps Institute of Oceanography argues that, by increasing atmospheric $CO_2$, humans are conducting a huge geophysical experiment on Earth. He proves that oceans will not absorb all the excess $CO_2$ produced by human technologies.

**A.D. 1979, Switzerland:** The World Climate Conference of meteorologists sounds the alarm for urgent international action against increasing $CO_2$ in the atmosphere.

**A.D. 1992, United States:** Many scientists blame Hurricane Andrew on climate change.

**A.D. 1997, Japan:** The United Nations-sponsored Kyoto Protocol is signed by eighty-four countries over the next two years. Governments that ratify the protocol commit to cut greenhouse-gas emissions, including $CO_2$, by at least 5.2% by 2012. The United States is the only major industrialized country to sign and then not ratify the protocol.

**A.D. 2000, Greenland:** Scientists studying air bubbles caught in glacier ice cores find that atmospheric levels of $CO_2$ have increased from 280 to 370 parts per million in just over two hundred years.

**A.D. 2001, United States:** NASA publishes photographs of over two thousand glaciers worldwide, which show that most have shrunk hundreds of meters over less than forty years. The photos spark public debate – are the glaciers retreating from natural or human-induced global warming?

**A.D. 2002, Antarctica:** Ice from the Larsen B ice shelf – 3,200 km² – falls off the continent and into the sea. Many – but not all – scientists consider this a result of global warming.

**A.D. 2004, Iceland:** The International Arctic Research Center reports that sea ice covers 10% less area than it did thirty years before and is only half as thick. Again, public debate erupts over what this means.

**A.D. 2004, Canada:** The government initiates a challenge to citizens to reduce their greenhouse-gas emissions by one tonne a year to help meet the Kyoto Protocol. The One-Tonne Challenge is canceled for lack of public interest in 2006.

**A.D. 2006, United States:** Former Vice President Al Gore releases his film documentary *An Inconvenient Truth*, explaining climate change and addressing the arguments of those who still deny global warming.

**A.D. 2008, Planet Earth:** The U.S. Climate Data Center declares that ten of the past thirteen years have been the warmest ever recorded.

**A.D. 2020, Planet Earth:** Will humans have started to turn down the global thermostat?

# INDEX